Theme Author Genre Similarity

Literarische Texte für den Englischunterricht der Sekundarstufe II
Herausgeber: Prof. Dr. Albert-Reiner Glaap

ROGER HALL

MULTIPLE CHOICE

Herausgegeben von
Prof. Dr. Albert-Reiner Glaap

Cornelsen

Multiple Choice

Verlagsredaktion
Neil Porter

Technische Umsetzung
Matthias Fuchs

Umschlagbild
John Dunne, Ashby Magna, Leics.

1. Auflage Druck 6 5 4 Jahr 2000 99 98

Alle Drucke dieser Auflage können im Unterricht nebeneinander verwendet werden.

Druck: Adolph Fürst & Sohn, Berlin

ISBN 3-464-66571-2

Bestellnummer 665712

gedruckt auf säurefreiem Papier,
umweltschonend hergestellt aus chlorfrei gebleichten Faserstoffen

Contents

Abbreviations

adj.	adjective	infml.	informal
adv.	adverb	n.	noun
AE	American English	o.s.	oneself
BE	British English	pl.	plural
cf.	confer	pron.	pronunciation
derog.	derogatory	sg.	singular
e.g.	for example	sb.	somebody
esp.	especially	sl.	slang
etc.	and so on	sth.	something
fml.	formal	usu.	usually
idm.	idiom	v.	verb

Roger Hall and *Multiple Choice*

The Play in the Making

In 1982, I and my wife took our children, Pip (short for Philippa) (10) and Simon (8) out of school for the year. We planned to spend the year travelling, starting off in the USA. Reactions from friends and teachers were interesting. It was our friends whose first response was, "What about their schooling?" The teachers, on the other hand, said, "Great idea. Don't worry about their schooling – they'll make it up with no problems."

I firmly believed that they would learn a great deal more from the experience of travelling though this wasn't my motive – my motive was selfish pleasure. Travel is the best drug I know.

In the USA we bought a mobile home (tacky, but practical) and set off south from Los Angeles, drove east across the southern border, and then up the East Coast as far as Washington, DC. It was a magic time. The first glimpse into the Grand Canyon; hearing coyotes howling at night; Texas; New Orleans; scuttling turtles at Myrtle Beach; seeing the Fonz's Jacket in a museum in Washington.

10 **schooling:** the education one receives at school 13–14 **make sth. up:** (here) catch up on sth. 16 **a great deal:** a lot 22 **tacky:** in poor taste 27 **glimpse:** short, incomplete view of sth. 30 **scuttle:** run with short, quick steps · **turtle:** (Wasser)Schildkröte 31 **Fonz's Jacket:** black leather jacket worn by the protagonist of the American TV series *Happy Days*

Who is Roger Hall?

- born in Woodford Wells, Essex, in 1939
- went to New Zealand at the age of 19
- worked for an insurance company for two years
- graduated from Victoria University in Wellington with an M.A. degree and was a teacher for three years
- wrote reviews for the *Listener*
- worked in the Department of Education
- wrote satirical sketches and scripts for television
- first play *Glide Time* (1976)
- some of his plays are not only popular *Down Under* (i.e. in Australia and New Zealand), but also in Europe and the United States
- Roger Hall is married and has a daughter and a son
- teaches as a Teaching Fellow at the University of Otago in Dunedin, South Island

The only education (Oh alright, they did a bit of Maths *occasionally*) was my reading aloud to them at least once every day (and quite often more): *The Cricket in Times Square, The Rats of Nimh, The Master Puppeteer; The Mouse and His Child* …

On the way, we stopped off at New Mexico State University, Las Cruces, where I was to give a couple of lectures. On the staff there was Mark Medoff, a wonderful playwright who had written *When Ya Comin' Back Red Ryder*, and *Children of a Lesser God*. He asked me if I would be interested in returning to Las Cruces to be a guest artist for their spring semester the following year. I would be required to do some teaching, and to write a play which their drama department would present. Naturally, I accepted (the year away now joyfully extended to 16 months). Our travels continued: to London to stay with my mother, and from there we travelled to various parts of the UK and to Crete; and then to Washington, DC, where we were to spend four months before going to Las Cruces in January. It was in Washington that I began to write the play.

I read several books by John Holt, and the one that stimulated me most was *Teach Your Own*, a handbook for those parents who did not wish to send their children to a school but to teach them at home.

The main issues that intrigued me were two: 1) who has the greater right to educate a child – the state or the parent? 2) what were the difficulties and practicalities of educating a child at home? I promptly solved the difficulties of having our children at home by sending Pip and Simon to school, the nearest public school, where 95% of the pupils and staff were black and where my two NZ children were made very welcome (I said my motivation was selfish).

Back in NZ I was to be asked why I had set the play in the USA and not in New Zealand. The first, and simplest, answer was that it was to have its première in the USA, acted by American students. The second was that I wanted it to be dramatic and therefore I needed the stakes to be high. I wanted it to be credible that Margie, Paul's mother, could be sent to prison, and that she was prepared to take that risk. In New Zealand, parents who teach their children at home may not always have an easy time of it (in fact, there is a national correspondence school that copes with most cases), no one has yet

5–8 **The Cricket in Times Square, The Rats of Nimh, The Master Puppeteer, The Mouse and His Child:** literature for children
21 **require sth. of sb.:** expect sth. from sb.

6 **intrigue sb.:** fascinate sb.

been sent to prison over the issue. In some states of the USA, parents *have* been imprisoned. So it made sense to set it in an unspecified state of the USA.

The more research I did for the play, the more excited I became by the issues it raised. Motivation – how hard it is to be motivated at school compared to those occasions when we want to learn. (Those adults who learnt more French in three months than they had learnt in several years at school because they wanted to learn it.) Learning by doing. Who do we learn best from – peers or teachers?

We moved from Washington to New Mexico, driving for seven days in a tiny Datsun station wagon, so crammed that Simon's head was jammed up against the car roof. I apologised to him for the conditions. "It's OK," he said. "It's better than school." (Hey! This reinforced some of the things I was going to say in the play.) At Las Cruces (a greater contrast from Washington is hard to imagine) I settled down to write the play. There followed the traditional trauma of auditions, rows over casting, changes of director, numerous re-writes, arguments over the title (it was presented there as *None of the Above*) – it was a happy time.

The play was very well received, and on some evenings the audience remained behind and argued over the issues the play raised – there was no doubt the piece stimulated argument.

It went to England, starred Susannah York in an out-of-town try-out, but failed to transfer to the West End. The play that I perhaps felt most passionately about the issues it contained proved to be one of my least successful. And therein lies the clue to its failure. It was Sam Goldwyn who said "If you've got a message send a telegram". Maybe the message *does* get in the way of the play. But I still like it as a play.

Postscript: It is now 1992, ten years later. I am once more taking a year away from home, spending most of the time in London, but also travelling whenever possible. My wife and family are still with me. Pip, 20, is taking a year out from university, Simon, 18, left school at the end of last year and is having a break before he starts university. They are working in restaurants, travelling in Europe, going to the theatre, and rock concerts (more rock concerts than theatre), and writing a huge amount of letters to friends. I don't think their year is being wasted.

6 **research** (n.): detailed study 17 **peer:** person equal to another in rank, status, age, etc. 21 **crammed:** packed too full 21–22 **be jammed up against sth.:** be pushed up against sth. 25 **reinforce sth.:** underline sth., make sth. stronger 29 **settle down to do sth.:** prepare to concentrate on doing sth. 31 **row** [raʊ]: noisy quarrel or difference of opinion

9 **star sb.:** have sb. in an important role 16 **clue** [kluː]: explanation

To
Marjorie Atlas
and the staff and students of the Theatre Arts Department,
New Mexico State University – with thanks.

April, 1983

Characters

Margie Hughes	solo parent, in her 30s
Paul Hughes	her son, aged 14
Betty Davidson	friend and neighbor of Margie
Mrs. Powell	School Principal
Miss Palmer	School Teacher
Grandmother	Margie's mother
Mr. Bronski	Superintendent (Administration) of Schools
Gordon Hughes	Paul's father, Margie's ex-husband
Mr. Akerman	Margie's boss
Roberto Mendez	aged about 17
School Attendance Officer	
Harris	Chairman of the School Board
Julia Beyer	Board Member
Kramer	Board Member
Sedillo	Board Member

A city on the coast of the USA.
Time: the present.

The set should be non-representational, with a minimum of chairs, tables, etc. Most of the practical props, such as the car and the sewing machine, should be imagined by the audience, with the actors miming whenever appropriate.

18 **school board:** group of people who control the policy of the school

ROGER HALL

Multiple Choice

Act One / Scene One

*[*MARGIE *talking directly to the audience.]*

MARGIE: Being a parent … it's making a million decisions, isn't it? Each decision open to debate, to doubt. What time bedtime? How much allowance? What programs on TV are not suitable.
Give a short smack, or a long lecture?
Because I said so!
Eating all those peas, and the value of money.
Hit back or lie low? Own up but don't tell. Do as you're told or speak out?
Black and white constantly merging into gray.
Paradox, irony, compromise …
Mostly, it's watching them swim in a cold sea, and we wait on the shore holding a towel. And day by day, they get out a bit further …
In the end, all you can do is what seems right at the time. And you have to live with that.

Act One / Scene Two

[At home. Evening. PAUL *lying on bed reading.* MARGIE *enters carrying bag of groceries. Puts them on table.]*

MARGIE: Hi!

PAUL: Hi!

MARGIE: Any phone calls?

PAUL: No.

*[*MARGIE *looks through the mail. Nothing of interest. Takes groceries through to kitchen area, returns with a drink.]*

MARGIE: Aren't you going to come out and say "Hallo" to the Aged P?

*[*PAUL *comes to his door and stands there.]*

4 **allowance** [ə'laʊəns]: pocket money 5 **smack** (n.): Klaps 8 **own up:** admit one did sth. bad
23 **Aged P** [ˌeɪdʒəd 'piː]: Aged Parent

Paul: Good evening. Bonsoir. Buenas noches. *[He moves to go back to his bed.]*

Margie: Hey, Berlitz! Come and talk to me! You don't know what it's like out there. Being in adult company all day, enough to drive a person neurotic – downtown neurosis.

Paul: You want to give your "Hard Day at the Office" piece?

Margie: You bet I do. Breadwinner's privilege – half hour of moaning as soon as they're in the door.

Paul: OK.

Margie: First off there was the car. Ignition and brakes. So first I can't start the thing and then I can't stop it. Mr. Akerman runs around like a beheaded chicken when the new typesetting machine breaks down. Carol gives me her daily filibuster about darling little Tracey. Henry forgot we had a dinner date. So now I want to hear about the real world – Did you whitewash Aunt Polly's fence? Build a raft and sail it down the Mississippi? Anything interesting happen at school?

Paul: Someone put mouse droppings in Glen Garvey's lunch.

Margie: Is that it? The aesthetic highlight of the day – mouse shit?

Paul: Well, you never like my "Hard Day at School" speech: The teachers don't listen; the work's boring; half the other kids are barbarians.

Margie: As I've told you before – you're one of the lucky ones. *[She lights a cigarette.]*

Paul: Are you trying to smoke yourself to death?

Margie: Yes. On my desk there's a sign that says "Thank you for smoking".

[He looks at her for a moment.]

Paul: Do you know what the cilia are?

Margie: No, but I will any second now.

Paul: I was reading about it. They're the tiny hairs that keep the lungs clean. Nicotine paralyzes them. Also nicotine makes the sac walls of the lung overstretch –

Margie: This isn't good enough, Paul.

Paul: What?

Margie: This continual interest in the human body. Mine in particular. If you're not careful, you'll end up being a doctor.

Paul: Wouldn't you like that?

Margie: Heaven forbid.

10 **ignition:** Zündung 12 **beheaded:** with one's head cut off 13 **filibuster** (AE): long, slow speech 15 **Aunt Polly:** Tom Sawyer's stepmother in Mark Twain's novel *Tom Sawyer* · **raft** [ræft; BE rɑːft]: floating platform made from large pieces of wood; allusion to Mark Twain's novel *Huckleberry Finn*, in which Huckleberry Finn and his friend Jim, who is a black slave, build a raft and sail it down the Mississippi

PAUL: Because Dad was?

MARGIE: Because you'd become a member of the most money-grubbing, status-seeking, self-satisfied profession in the world.

PAUL: OK.

MARGIE *[Sincerely]:* You be exactly what you want to be, kiddo. But there's no hurry to decide.

PAUL: What's for dinner?

MARGIE: Pizza.

PAUL: Gross!

MARGIE: Well, I'm sorry, but when I get home I haven't the energy to cook. Pizza's quick and easy. And cheap. You feel so strongly about it, you cook.

PAUL: Too much homework.

MARGIE: What tonight?

PAUL: Science. Book report. Prepare a talk on a historical figure. About a million square roots.

MARGIE: And they say it's all geared to the space race.

PAUL *[Hesitantly]:* Actually … in math, Miss Palmer made me … that is, I –

[Door buzzer goes.]

MARGIE: Hallo.

BETTY: Betty.

MARGIE: Come on up.

*[*PAUL *goes into his room, starts work.* BETTY *enters carrying a dress.]*

BETTY: I want you to try it and see if it needs any alterations.

*[*MARGIE *tries on the dress.]*

MARGIE: It's time you had your own shop.

BETTY: Chuck'd never hear of it.

MARGIE: If he had any sense he'd give up his own job and set you up in business. This is great. All I want now is an occasion to wear it. Thanks, Betty, I'm really pleased with that. *[She writes out check.]* That's what we said, wasn't it?

BETTY: Thanks. Dean asked me to give these to Paul. Notes he took in class … he'll need them for homework, Dean said.

MARGIE: Paul! Betty's got some notes for you.

*[*PAUL *enters.]*

PAUL: Hey! That looks kinda neat!

2 **money-grubbing:** geldgierig 5 **kiddo** (sl.): friend 9 **gross** [grəʊs](sl.): disgusting 16 **square root:** Quadratwurzel 17 **gear sth. to sth. else:** orientate sth. to sth. else 18 **math** (AE): mathematics

BETTY: Thank you, Paul.

MARGIE: She designed it, too. What are you like at windbreakers? Paul needs a new one.

BETTY: I made the boys theirs.

PAUL: Did you make those?! They told me they were from Sears.

BETTY *[Laughs.]:* They hate wearing things I make. *[Handing over notes]* Dean said to give you these.

PAUL: Oh. Thanks.

MARGIE: Why didn't you take notes for yourself?

PAUL: Cos Miss Logan made me miss science.

MARGIE: Why?!

PAUL: Because I told her about the Inuit. Half the class thought they still go around in kayaks and live in igloos and all that. I tried to tell her about when we were up there with Uncle David. She knows nothing, that woman. Thought I was being "smart".

MARGIE: And she made you miss science?

PAUL: She does that all the time. She keeps you out of a subject she thinks you like, as a punishment. I've missed three sessions on the computer.

MARGIE: Mad! Crazy! You go to school to –

BETTY: I must go! Chuck'll be home any second. *[To* PAUL*]* Come over real soon and I'll measure you for a windbreaker. Bye.

MARGIE: Bye, Betty, and thanks again.

*[*BETTY *leaves.]*

I better put the despised pizza on. *[She goes through to kitchen. Calling]* Tell me when twenty minutes is up.

*[*PAUL *sets his watch.]*

Forget homework for the time being – Let's read. *[About to read]* Listen, you'd say if you didn't want me to read, wouldn't you? If you feel you're past this … this sort of thing. You're not just doing it to humor the Aged P?

PAUL: No. But you don't tell anyone, do you?

MARGIE: Strictly *entre nous*. "CHAPTER FIVE, Nicholas starts for Yorkshire. Of his Leave-taking and his Fellow-Travellers, and what befell them on the Road. If tears dropped into a trunk were charms to preserve its

2 **windbreaker:** anorak 5 **Sears:** US chain store providing a mail order catalogue for farming people 12 **Inuit:** Canadian Native people sometimes referred to as "Eskimos" 15 **smart:** acting like sb. who knows everything 24 **despise sb./sth.:** dislike sb./sth. intensely 32 **entre nous** (French): between you and me 33 **befall sb.** (fml.): happen to sb. 34 **trunk:** large box used for carrying things on a journey · **charm:** small object said to bring good luck

owner from sorrow and misfortune, Nicholas Nickleby would have commenced his expedition under most –"

[Phone rings.]

That'll be Henry. *[Answers.]* Hallo. Mrs. Powell?

[Hearing who it is, PAUL *goes through to his room.]*

Yes? Yes ... He wouldn't ...? I see. Right, yes, I'll come and see you if you think it's ... Tomorrow will be fine. *[Rings off.]* Paul? Paul!

Act One / Scene Three

[Office of MRS. POWELL, *the School Principal.]*

POWELL: Come in, Mrs. Hughes, won't keep you a minute. Vera! No calls for fifteen minutes. Would you call the Board and tell them for the third time that we *have* sent in the immunization forms. Tell Mrs. Nicolls I'll see her tomorrow. And if that mad preacher calls again say *we* invite the speakers for Education Week and not the other way round. *[To* MARGIE*]* Thursdays ... madhouse. It is every day of the week, but specially Thursdays, don't ask me why. *[Giving* MARGIE *her attention at last]* Now ...?

MARGIE: You sent for me.

POWELL: Oh, yes, of course ... Paul. Not doing his homework for Miss Palmer. Vera! Page Shelley Palmer for me. It seems he got the idea from you.

MARGIE: Not exactly. But I have told him he should speak out against things he thinks are wrong.

POWELL: He thinks homework is wrong?

MARGIE: No. Only if it's a complete waste of time.

POWELL: It's never that, Mrs. Hughes. At the very least it's a discipline. When he goes on to high school, he's going to get a lot more than he does now, so he might as well get used to it.

MARGIE: That's like saying you should work part-time now, so you can get used to being retired.

POWELL: Wonderful! Suggest it to the Board. You know what's one of the most common complaints I get from parents? That we don't set enough homework. They want their kids to be working instead of wasting time watching TV or fooling around on the street.

1 **Nicholas Nickleby:** protagonist of the novel of the same name by Charles Dickens (1812–1870)
11 **immunization form:** form in which details of vaccinations (= Impfungen) received are listed
19 **page sb.:** call out sb.'s name over a loudspeaker

MARGIE: Whatever happened to childhood?

POWELL: There are the weekends.

*[*MISS PALMER *enters.]*

POWELL: Ah, Shelley, you know Mrs. Hughes?

[They acknowledge each other.]

POWELL: I think it would be best if you told us exactly what happened.

PALMER: I assigned the class forty square roots to do for homework Tuesday night. The next day Paul hadn't done them and when I asked him why he said it was because he could already do them so there wasn't any point in spending time on them.

POWELL: He really has to do the homework he's assigned.

MARGIE: There's a bit more to it than that. You did square roots in class on Monday and Paul got them all right. You assigned thirty to do for homework that night and he got those all right. You did more in class the next day and he got those all right. And then you go and set forty more that night. How many does he have to do to prove that he can do them?

PALMER: I know all that, but I have at least thirty kids in each class. I can't go setting different homework for each of them.

MARGIE: So why set it at all?! Either they can do square roots or they can't. If they can, then it's a waste of time; and if they can't, having to do forty of them is sheer misery.

POWELL: The point, Mrs. Hughes, is that Paul told Miss Palmer here in front of the whole class that he wasn't going to do the homework.

MARGIE: No, the point is the school's total inability to cope with kids as individuals.

[Pause.]

PALMER: I have to teach math to close to two hundred –

MARGIE: School's never been able to cope! Right from the first day. He learned to read before he went to school, and when he turned up in class and told the teacher she said "Oh no, now what are we going to do with you!" She made him go through all the pre-reading stuff. And sure enough, after a month, he couldn't read. Paul's above average – he's not gifted or exceptional at anything. But he reads a lot, we talk a lot, we've traveled, he's interested in a lot of things.

PALMER: If you knew what it was like to have kids in the class who know it all, or who have been everywhere.

MARGIE: Are you saying in taking Paul to places and talking to him about things, I've been making some sort of mistake! That I should have

7 assign sth.: give sth. as homework **24 cope with sb./sth.:** try to deal with sb./sth.

deliberately held him back. Is that the school motto – "Keeping Down with the Joneses"!

POWELL: We do the best we can under diff–

MARGIE *[In full cry]:* The playground's like a jungle. Everything from having your lunch stolen to racial hatred. Paul used to get roughed up because he wore glasses, or for reading in recess. And the teachers do nothing! For a time, he was having nightmares –

POWELL: Mrs. Hughes, I know how a mother feels. Especially when it's an only child. But all those things that have happened to Paul happen all the time. It's perfectly normal.

MARGIE *[Shouting]:* Yes, normal!! Don't you think that's frightening – that it's considered normal!!

[Slight pause.]

PALMER: Paul shouldn't have defied me in front of the whole class. And then, to say that his mother told him to –

POWELL: We'll see if we can work something out, but in the meantime, please get him to do the forty sums for Miss –

MARGIE: You realize she assigned him *another* forty as punishment.

POWELL: Well, whatever.

MARGIE: I can't ask him to do that.

POWELL: In cases like this, parents usually back us up.

[No reply.]

POWELL: Well, I'm sorry, I can't just let it pass. I have to suspend him.

MARGIE: Suspend him!

POWELL: We did it to another boy for something similar. So I have to do it for Paul.

MARGIE: See! Again! Unable to cope with individuals.

POWELL: I'm sorry. He can be re-admitted just as soon as he does them.

MARGIE: As far as I can tell, Paul isn't happy at school; and he doesn't seem to be learning much. There's not much point in his being here.

[So? Nothing new in that think MISS PALMER *and* MRS. POWELL.*]*

So I'm taking him out of school.

POWELL: What was that?

MARGIE: I'm taking him out of school. He can stay at home and do his work there.

PALMER: You can't do that, Mrs. Hughes. School's compulsory.

1–2 **keep down with the Joneses** (from **keep up with the Joneses**): be as good as the neighbours 5 **rough sb. up** (infml.): use physical violence against sb. 6 **recess** ['ri:ses](AE): break between the lessons 14 **defy sb.:** openly disobey sb. 21 **back sb. up:** help, support sb. 23 **suspend sb.:** forbid sb. to attend school 36 **compulsory:** that must be done

POWELL: The only way you can do that is if I give him an exemption.

MARGIE: Give him one then! You've just shown you don't want him in school. I'm sure he'll learn a damn sight more at home than he does here.

*[*MISS PALMER *and* MRS. POWELL *look at each other.]*

He can see the day out here – and that's the finish.

[She goes out. MISS PALMER *and* MRS. POWELL *relieved to see her go.]*

Act One / Scene Four

[At McDonald's. PAUL, MARGIE *and* GRANDMOTHER *find a place to sit.* GRANDMOTHER *looks at her food with little enthusiasm.]*

GRANDMOTHER: I find it hard to believe they've sold fifty million of these.

PAUL: Billion. Fifty thousand million.

GRANDMOTHER: It can only be a Russian plot … destroying America from within.

MARGIE: It's cheap and it's fast.

GRANDMOTHER: But the food, Margerie!

MARGIE: You can't have everything. I'm sorry, Mother, but it's a handy place to eat. And I'm very grateful you can take Paul at such short notice.

PAUL: I could have stayed at home.

MARGIE: Not for a whole weekend.

GRANDMOTHER: It's all very rushed.

MARGIE: I know, but when you get asked to go to New York by a man who has opera tickets, you go.

PAUL: It is Henry?

MARGIE: Of course.

PAUL *[To* GRANDMOTHER*]:* That's the scrawny one.

GRANDMOTHER: Now, Margerie, you've been avoiding this. Tell me, clearly, in words that even a grandmother can understand, why you have taken Paul out of school.

MARGIE: Because … public schools are the McDonald's of education.

GRANDMOTHER: That is a smart answer you've just thought up.

MARGIE: It's all right, Mother. He does his work during the day, and I shall go over it at night.

GRANDMOTHER: I thought keeping children at home was against the law.

1 **exemption:** special permission not to do sth. 3 **a damn sight more** (infml.): a great deal more 16 **handy** (infml.): convenient 17 **at short notice:** with little warning 20 **rush sth.:** do sth. in a hurry 25 **scrawny** ['skrɑːniː; BE 'skrɔnɪ]: thin

MARGIE: We have to get an exemption. Paul's principal won't give us one, so we're applying to the District Board.

GRANDMOTHER: You've rushed into it, haven't you? Without any thought, any preparation. It's a fad, isn't it? A trend.

MARGIE: No!

GRANDMOTHER: If home births had been the in-thing when Paul was born, you'd have had him in the sitting room with half the neighborhood watching.

MARGIE: That's not true –

GRANDMOTHER: You're always galloping off in all directions.

MARGIE *[Wearily]:* I took him out of school because he wasn't learning anything –

GRANDMOTHER: All right, but apart from the school subjects – which I cannot believe you're capable of teaching him, what about all the other things school teaches you – the social values?

MARGIE *[At last able to go on the attack]:* Oh, the social values! Shall I tell you the social values I learned at that good private school you sent me to? I learned to gang up on other kids, and to sneer at the girls who had less money than we did. I learned to swear and to talk dirty. I learned how to cheat at lessons and lie to teachers. I had my first cigarette at school and my first taste of alcohol. And once, I even went shoplifting. Those are the social values I learned at school, Mother.

PAUL: I know most of them already.

MARGIE: And nowadays you can add to that list, learning how and where to get drugs. So please don't suggest that by keeping Paul out of school, I'm socially depriving him.

PAUL: Don't forget the headlice.

GRANDMOTHER: Tell me this – did you go and talk to the school first? Tell them you were worried about Paul's –

MARGIE *[Standing]:* It'll be all right! I should have done it years ago. Paul is much happier at home, and he's working really hard. Anything either of you want from New York?

4 **fad:** short-lived interest in sth. 18 **gang up on sb.:** come together to insult and attack sb. · **sneer at sb.:** show contempt for sb. 19 **swear** [swer; BE sweə]: use bad language 20 **cheat:** (here) copy other students' schoolwork 21 **shoplift:** steal things from a shop 26 **deprive sb.:** take sth. away from sb. 27 **headlouse** (pl. **headlice**): small insect living in a person's hair

Act One / Scene Five

*[*BRONSKI *is dictating a letter while simultaneously* MARGIE *is reading it.]*

BRONSKI: Mrs. Margerie Hughes, 3142 Wilson Ave., Apartment 3, Zip 4006. Dear Mrs. Hughes, Referring to your application for your son to be exempt from attending Glenn Junior High School, I have to advise you that we are unable to grant such an exemption. Exemptions from attending public school are normally granted only in the cases where parental religious beliefs are in conflict with the school system or in medical cases where in some way the school system cannot cater for the particular requirements of the child concerned. As you do not fall into either category, I regret that we cannot grant you an exemption.

Under the laws of the State, school attendance is compulsory for all persons between the ages of 6 and 16, and therefore you are required to reinstate your son in school at the earliest possible date.

Yours etc.

C. F. Bronski, Superintendent Administration, Redwood County Education District.

MARGIE *[Almost at end]:* Yeah, yeah, yeah. *[Tears up letter.]*

Act One / Scene Six

[At BETTY'S. BETTY *on sewing machine.* PAUL *watching.]*

BETTY: Here ... try it on.

*[*PAUL *tries on the new windbreaker. She makes some adjustments.]*

BETTY: That should be OK in a couple of days.

PAUL: Where did you learn to sew?

BETTY: At home. There was an old machine us kids could use.

PAUL: Ma never makes anything.

BETTY: Oh well ... I was never any good at school. It's not that difficult you know. Like to have a try?

PAUL: Yes, please.

BETTY: Here. *[She puts in piece of old material.]* Try some of the different stitches.

PAUL: Hey! It's amazing.

2 zip (AE): postcode **9 cater for sth.:** satisfy a particular need for sth. · **requirement:** need
14 reinstate sb.: (here) send back

BETTY: Try some more.

[He does so.]

There you are – an instant sampler. How's the school work going?

PAUL: At home?

BETTY: Yes. Chuck says no kid learns unless he's made to. Don't you get lonely?

PAUL: No. A bit. It's kind of hard – making yourself do it. I mean, I can do all the work I'd do in a school day pretty quickly – but because I've got all day to do it ... I don't know.

BETTY: If you ever get lonesome, you can always come here. I like having someone to talk to, too. Like to stay for lunch?

PAUL: Yes, please!

BETTY: Good. Here... Reckon you could make this? *[Shows him a pattern.]* This tote bag? The pieces are all cut out; all it needs is sewing up.

PAUL: What if I make a mistake?

BETTY: No matter, I can always undo it. You start on it, while I put something on for lunch.

Act One / Scene Seven

[At home. MARGIE *sorting out a heap of bills.]*

MARGIE: Damn stupid bills – I can't work it out.

PAUL: Want me to help?

MARGIE: No. Thanks.

PAUL: Are we in debt?

MARGIE: Always. Oh God, how do people manage?

*[*PAUL *looks through the bills.]*

PAUL: Wow! Visa!

MARGIE: How else could we have got to Alaska? How else can we get to Mexico?

PAUL: Mexico!!

MARGIE: Unless you can think of someplace better.

PAUL: No. Wow!

MARGIE: Might have to go to the bank for Mexico. Again.

3 instant (adj.): made very quickly · **sampler:** Stickmustertuch **13 reckon** (infml.): think; suppose **14 tote bag:** large bag to tote (i.e. carry) things around **23 be in debt:** verschuldet sein

PAUL: How much do we owe altogether?

MARGIE: Oh, Paul, I don't know. The bank, the car, the credit cards. Do you think Visa would take American Express?

PAUL: But if we got another loan, it'd only increase the monthly payments. We'd be worse off than ever.

MARGIE: None of your childish logic here, thank you. I don't know. Listen, sorry I mentioned Mexico – don't count on it, huh? *[She pushes bills aside.]* Let's forget this and wallow in Dickens.

[Door buzzer goes. PAUL *answers.]*

PAUL: Hallo?

[Voice. We can't hear distinctly.]

PAUL: Oh, er, hi …

[Voice continues.]

PAUL: OK. *[Presses release button.]* It's Dad.

MARGIE: Your father?

PAUL: Yes.

MARGIE *[Panicking]:* Jesus Christ, he's supposed to make an appointment for a visit. You shouldn't let him – ohhhh. *[She rushes towards bedroom, rushes back to sweep bills off table. Removes drink and ashtray, too. Just gets into bedroom as* GORDON *enters. He has a bunch of flowers and a package in hand. He and* PAUL *shake hands awkwardly.]*

GORDON: You're growing up.

PAUL: That's the idea.

*[*GORDON *hands him package, from its shape a football.* PAUL *unwraps it.]*

PAUL *[Embarrassed]:* Thanks.

GORDON: I wasn't sure if you played or not.

PAUL: Soccer, sometimes.

GORDON: Oh. Score many points?

PAUL: Goals. No.

GORDON: Well, you'll have to come up home, take you to see the Patriots.

PAUL: Yeah.

[Pause.]

GORDON: How's school?

PAUL: Er … It's, you know, much the same.

*[*MARGIE *sweeps in, having groomed herself quickly, and manages a dignified entrance.]*

MARGIE: Gordon.

4 **loan:** borrowed money 8 **wallow in sth.:** in etwas schwelgen 30 **the Patriots:** American football team 35 **groom oneself:** make oneself look neat and tidy

GORDON: Listen, sorry to have called without checking first, but I was in town and I – here. *[Hands her flowers.]*

MARGIE: Thank you.

GORDON: I don't think I'd have recognized Paul.

MARGIE: Well, it's been a long time.

GORDON *[Controlling himself]:* Yes. One of the reasons I called was to suggest Paul might like to come up to Boston for a weekend.

PAUL: Er ...

GORDON: Whenever suits you. You don't have to decide now. But I thought while I was in town, perhaps we could go out for a meal. Or a movie. Just you and me.

MARGIE *[Correcting]:* "You and I".

PAUL: Er ... yes ... er ...

MARGIE: Perhaps your father and I could talk alone for a bit.

PAUL: Sure. Yes. *[He goes through to room.]*

*[*MARGIE *waits until* PAUL *is out of earshot.]*

MARGIE: You're supposed to make an appointment.

GORDON: Whenever I have, you've always managed to break it. This way, I thought at least I'd have a chance of seeing Paul.

[She tries to cool down.]

MARGIE: You didn't say why you were in town.

GORDON: Dermatology conference.

MARGIE: Really? What's the keynote address? "How to Make More Money Out of Herpes"?

*[*GORDON *doesn't reply.]*

And how's Thing?

GORDON: Angela stayed at home.

MARGIE: As she's always done. Can't have those hands soiled by anything as vulgar as work, can we?

GORDON *[Wearily]:* God, Margie, can't you ever be –

MARGIE: No, I can't.

GORDON: You're still so bitter.

MARGIE: I've been bitter every single day since you left. God, it still makes me angry. I see you through all those years of study, I have to give up my studies, we live in stinking little apartments, you blithely come round Europe with us on my folks' money, and then you leave me for the first girl that comes along waving her butt at you.

16 **out of earshot:** too far away to hear what is said 22 **dermatology** [- - ˎ - -]: branch of medicine dealing with the human skin 28 **soil sth.:** make sth. dirty 35 **blithe** [blaɪð]: happy and carefree 37 **butt** (sl.): bottom, backside

GORDON: It wasn't like –

MARGIE: I used to think that doctors, seeing so much female flesh each day, would be immune. But oh, no, flash a bit of boob at them and they're away.

GORDON: If it makes it easier for you to believe that –

MARGIE: I will say this for you, Gordon. Your timing was perfect. You ditched me just the right time; before there was any property to divide. So I got half of nothing. *[Indicates the room.]* You like this place? You like to try living here? Would Angela condescend to place a languid toe in these doors? She wouldn't even lower the window of her Mercedes to look at us.

GORDON: No wonder he never wants to come and see me. If this is the way you talk about me. *[This hits her.]*

MARGIE: No. No, I don't. I think I'm fair to you. Mind you, he's aware of my thinly veiled contempt for the medical profession. No, not even that's true. I don't even bother with the veil.

[They both smile at this form of honesty.]

GORDON: How's he doing?

MARGIE: Great. He's a great kid.

GORDON: You still read to him?

MARGIE: Oh yes! Every night. Right now it's *Nicholas Nickleby*.

GORDON: Yeah? I saw it on TV. Some of it. You were always reading to him. Even on holiday; through Europe.

MARGIE: Well, it paid off. He reads anything he can get his hands on now.

GORDON: I bet.

MARGIE: That fool of a school complained he was reading too much! That's one of the reasons why I took him –

GORDON: What?

MARGIE: Nothing.

GORDON: "Took him …" Took him to what? To a psychologist?

MARGIE: No, no, nothing like that.

GORDON: Margie, I'm entitled to know.

[Pause, longish.]

MARGIE: I wasn't happy with the way things were going at school so I … I took him out. I'm teaching him at home.

GORDON: Oh my God.

MARGIE: He wasn't learning any–

3 **boob** (sl.): female breast 7 **ditch sb.** (infml.): abandon, leave sb. 9 **condescend:** sich herablassen · **languid** ['læŋgwɪd]: slow-moving 15 **veil sth.:** cover sth. with a veil (= Schleier) 32 **be entitled to sth.:** have a right to sth.

GORDON: What are you trying to do, ruin his life? I mean in the first place it's against the law, isn't it?

MARGIE: I'm seeing the Board about an exemp–

GORDON: This is typical of you; up in the air stuff.

MARGIE: He's my child; I'm doing what I think best for him.

GORDON: He's my child, too.

MARGIE: Christ, it's a little late in the day for signs of parental concern, isn't it? When you were still with us, you were hardly ever around. Paul thought that a father was something attached to a beeper.

[GORDON *reacts.*]

He was being bullied at school! For reading.

GORDON: So? Make him fight back! He can't run behind your skirts all his life.

MARGIE: The main thing was he wasn't learning at school.

GORDON: Is he learning at home?

MARGIE: Yes!

GORDON: I wonder.

MARGIE: All right, all right. I'll show you. I have absolute trust in him – that he works better at home than he ever did at school. Paul!

[PAUL *enters.*]

GORDON: You told me you were in school. You told a lie.

PAUL: No, I didn't. You asked me how school was and I told you.

GORDON: You said …

PAUL: I said it was much the same, which it is.

MARGIE: Your father needs convincing that you do work at home. I want you to show him what you did today.

PAUL *[Dismayed]:* Today?

MARGIE: And yesterday.

PAUL: Well, I did some reading and, … er … some social studies.

GORDON: What?

PAUL: The … the … Inuit.

GORDON: Show me what you've done.

PAUL: I didn't write anything; just read about them. I did some math.

MARGIE: Show your father.

[PAUL *gets some papers.*]

PAUL: Calculating the volume of a cylinder.

9 **beeper** (AE) = (BE) **bleeper:** Piepser 11 **bully sb.:** frighten and hurt sb. 27 **dismay sb.:** shock and discourage sb.

*[*Gordon *looks at the work.]*

Gordon: Not very many. And I think you'd have to agree, a mess. *[Hands it to* Margie.*]*

Paul *[Realizing he's let* Margie *down]:* Sorry. *[He goes back to his room.]*

Gordon: You call this working better at home?

Margie: The volume of a cylinder! What is the point?

Gordon: Margie.

Margie: I suppose you're going to tell me you have to calculate the volume of a cylinder every single day of your working life.

Gordon: You cannot say he's working better at home.

Margie: I'll make sure I'll supervise him better.

Gordon *[Gently]:* Don't make him suffer for one of your ideas. He has to go back to school.

Margie: I never could explain things to you. Make you understand how I felt about things.

[Pause.]

Gordon *[No reply. Goes to* Paul*'s room.]:* Bye, Paul.

Paul: Bye.

Gordon: Think about Boston.

Paul: OK.

*[*Gordon *goes.]*

Margie: Paul!

[Reluctantly he comes out of his room. She indicates him to sit.]

Know how I imagined all this would be? Your staying home from school? You zipping through a week's math in a day. Rushing off to the library to find out all about the Ancient Egyptians. Writing stories and poems full of fire. My coming home and you hardly being able to pour out all the things you learned during the day. And what do I find! This … this … I wouldn't accept this from a third grader. *[She rips it up.]* What do you *do* all day? *[Silence.]* Well? *[Silence.]* You made me look like a fool!

Paul: I try…to do some work, but at home it seems…pointless. Irrelevant.

Margie: I have to work all day and then come home and feed you and when I do come home I find this place a pig sty, the dishes aren't done, and now I find you haven't even done any work!

Paul: What are you going to do about it?! Keep me in?! Make me do 80 square roots?!

23 **reluctant:** unwilling 25 **zip through sth.:** finish sth. extremely quickly 29 **third grader:** pupil aged about 7 or 8 34 **pig sty:** place where pigs are kept; complete mess

Margie: You said schoolwork was irrelevant, right? OK. *[She grabs bills.]* These bills sorted out, checks written, ready for me to sign, my exact financial situation worked out – math. Kitchen, bedroom, living room – kept clean and tidy. Bathroom and toilet cleaned twice a week –

Paul: The toilet!

Margie: The evening meal cooked by you three times a week – domestic science.

Paul: But that –

Margie: You want to come with me to Mexico next year, you earn the money to pay for it – social studies.

Paul: Aw, Ma –

Margie: Sorry, kiddo, you had your chance for freedom, and you blew it.

Act One / Scene Eight

*[*Margie *at work.]*

Margie: So I said, OK fine, that's the way it is, you do all the housework. And he's doing it. School work comes as a light relief after all that cleaning. The school? They've just left us alone. I got this bland form letter from the Board, but I'm sure they've forgotten all about us. Try it with Tracey, Carol – she'd love it.

*[*Akerman *bursts in trailing galley proofs.]*

Akerman: Ladies, ladies, may I remind you that we are not a firm of gentlemen publishers, but the back-alley sweat shop of jobbing printers. We are not producing fine-bound editions of the work of Miss Austen, but the grubby, ill-written newsletters of half the service clubs in this city; insincere Christmas greetings from business firms; and umpteenth unrepeatable offers from merchandising emporia. All mundane no doubt to ladies of your breeding, but they do pay the bills. Meanwhile we have Pearl and Patrick in paste-up waiting for clean copy, and what do we get from you ladies but more mistakes than from a kid with his first printing outfit!

6–7 **domestic science:** study of the skills of housekeeping 16 **bland:** unexciting 16–17 **form letter:** standardized letter 19 **trail sth.:** hinter sich herziehen · **galley proof:** sheet of paper on which a printer prints a book so that mistakes can be corrected before it is divided into pages 21 **back-alley:** small back street · **sweat shop:** factory where workers are employed for long hours and low pay 23 **grubby:** dirty 25 **umpteenth:** countless · **merchandising emporium** (pl. **emporia**): large shop selling many different things 26 **mundane** [mʌn'deɪn]: ordinary, not very exciting 27 **paste-up:** (hier) Herstellungsabteilung · **clean copy:** letzte von Fehlern gereinigte Fassung

Most of this doesn't apply to you, Mrs. Tyler, but you *[To* MARGIE*]* seem to be doing your best to get yourself into the *Guinness Book of World Records*.

MARGIE: Sorry.

AKERMAN: A year ago, the firm you were with went down the tubes. "Be grateful for anything", you said. And I, in my infinite mercy, took you on. Now, I ask myself –

MARGIE: I'm sorry. I …

AKERMAN: Yes?

[No reply.]

[Gently] Just … keep them down to a minimum, OK?

Act One / Scene Nine

[At home. PAUL *is at work, using calculator, with bills beside him. Door buzzer goes.]*

VOICE: Your grandmother. *[A moment later, she enters.]*

PAUL: Hi, Grandma.

GRANDMOTHER: How are you?

PAUL: Fine.

GRANDMOTHER: You look busy.

PAUL: I'm sorting out the bills – it's one of my jobs.

GRANDMOTHER: Like a hand?

PAUL: No, I can do it.

*[*GRANDMOTHER *looks around.]*

GRANDMOTHER: This place is a mess. I know it's not my business but it truly is.

PAUL: That's my job, too. I'll finish these, then I'll –

GRANDMOTHER: What *is* she doing? Trying to make you into the perfect little housewife.

PAUL: I don't mind it.

GRANDMOTHER: Well, I do! Sorry, but I am entitled to the occasional bellow from the sideline. *[Paces around.]* It annoys me to see you wasting your time when you should be –

PAUL: I'm not wasting time! I'm –

5 **go down the tubes** (infml.): go bankrupt 30 **bellow** (n.): loud shout · **sideline:** line around a playing field, football pitch, etc.

GRANDMOTHER: All right, all right. I'll say no more. If you want help – lessons, housework, anything – let me know. I presume I am allowed to make a cup of coffee. *[She moves to kitchen.]*

PAUL: Could you let me have three thousand dollars?

GRANDMOTHER: Three thousand –

PAUL: As a loan – I'd pay interest.

GRANDMOTHER: Are you in some sort of trouble? Is it drugs?

PAUL: Ma owes about $3000 altogether. There's the car, she's paying 14% on that; and the loan from the bank. But the main thing is Visa – she thought she was paying 18%, but I've checked and it's 2 1/2% a month. That's 30% a year. She's got no idea.

GRANDMOTHER: She never did have.

PAUL: She's paying $12 a week on interest alone. If I borrowed three thousand off you, I could pay it all off. If I paid you ten percent, that'd be only $6 a week.

GRANDMOTHER: Where did you learn about all this?

PAUL: I went to the bank. The girl there –

GRANDMOTHER: Woman!

PAUL: Woman there thought I was doing it for a school project, but when I told her the whole situation, she was very helpful. I'm going to open an account there.

GRANDMOTHER: Well ... I owe you an apology. If you've found out that much about money at your age, I can't say you've been wasting your time. I'll let you have the money ... it'll take a few days, OK.

PAUL: Thanks. But you won't tell –

GRANDMOTHER: Our secret. Well, hausfrau, what other jobs do you have to do?

PAUL: Cook the meal.

GRANDMOTHER: Really? And what are you planning for tonight?

PAUL: Pizza.

GRANDMOTHER: Pizza!

PAUL: It's quick and easy. And cheap.

GRANDMOTHER: Well, let your ancient grandmother show you something. I will show you how to prepare a casserole.

PAUL: A casserole?

GRANDMOTHER: It sounds so much better than Irish Stew. And once you've prepared it, it lasts for days and days ...

6 **interest** (n.): Zinsen 36 **Irish Stew:** hot pot with mutton, onions and other vegetables

Act One / Scene Ten

[Outside. PAUL *enters with oil, wrench, baking tin, and car maintenance book. He studies the book, then crawls under the car, and undoes the nut. Gives a cry as oil begins to come out. His hand is reaching out for the baking tin which is out of reach, when* ROBERTO *walks by. He sees what is happening and hands* PAUL *the tin.]*

PAUL: Thanks.

ROBERTO: Sure.

PAUL *[Emerging from under the car]:* I've never done this before.

ROBERTO: Change the oil? Nothing to it.

PAUL *[Checking the book]:* Now I've got the oil out, where do I put it in?

*[*ROBERTO *points.* PAUL *unscrews the cap and is about to pour in oil.]*

ROBERTO: Your new oil gonna join the old?

PAUL: What?

ROBERTO: Fix the plug underneath.

PAUL: Oh. *[Laughs.]* Thanks. *[He does so then pours in the oil.]*

ROBERTO: Hey, aren't you gonna clean the filter?

PAUL: The filter?

ROBERTO: Too late now, man.

PAUL *[Handing him the book]:* Show me.

ROBERTO: I don't need that. What you doing that for? Can't your Dad do it?

PAUL: I haven't got one. At least, he's in Boston. I'm trying to save us some money – what's a lube job worth? Ten, fifteen dollars.

ROBERTO: Lube job you gotta have a grease gun, grease all the points, clean the filter.

PAUL: Is it hard?

ROBERTO: Easy – gotta have the right tools though. What else needs doing to this thing?

PAUL: The brakes need doing. And there's something wrong with the ignition.

ROBERTO: I'll be right back. You get the rear wheels jacked up. *[He goes.]*

*[*PAUL *gets the jack out. Puts it in position and cautiously turns the handle.* ROBERTO *returns with tool box.]*

Hey! Not there, you put the jack there it'll come right through the floor. *[He puts it in the right place, jacks it up. Opens up toolbox.]*

1 **wrench** (AE) = (BE) **spanner:** Schraubenschlüssel · **baking tin:** container in which a cake is made 1–2 **car maintenance book:** book which describes how to repair and look after a car 2 **nut:** Schraubenmutter 14 **plug:** Stöpsel 22 **lube** (sl.) = **lubrication:** Schmierung 30 **rear** (adj.): back · **jack sth. up:** lift up sth. with a jack (= Wagenheber)

PAUL: Those all yours?

ROBERTO: Uhuh.

*[*PAUL *offers* ROBERTO *the manual.]*

Don't need it. *[He takes off wheels to check brakes.]*

PAUL: You a mechanic?

ROBERTO: Got no job.

PAUL: I thought mechanics get jobs anywhere.

ROBERTO: No qualifications. The shoes are shot. I expect the front ones are the same. The garage give you a quote?

PAUL: $105. Here, I'll show you –

ROBERTO: Sounds right. I'll do it for you for sixty. Ignition – I'll charge you what time it takes to fix, $5 an hour, that's cheap, OK? And I'll give it a free tune up – love to tune these things, OK?

PAUL: I don't know.

[Pause.]

I mean, what if …?

ROBERTO: I mess it up? My brother works in a garage; he gets the parts cheap; anything too serious we take it there, he'll fix it up, OK?

PAUL: I'd want a written quote.

ROBERTO: Sure, sure, you write it, I'll sign it.

*[*PAUL *gets pen and paper and does so.]*

PAUL: Can I watch you do it?

ROBERTO: Sure.

*[*PAUL *hands him paper.]*

PAUL: You better put your address up the top.

ROBERTO: You do it, my hands are dirty. Roberto Mendez, 2214 Garfield, just round the corner.

*[*PAUL *adds address and hands it to him.* ROBERTO *signs.* PAUL *slowly realizes, and is amazed.]*

PAUL: Can't you read?

[Pause.]

ROBERTO: I get by.

8 **the shoes are shot** (AE sl.): the brakes are worn out 9 **quote** (n.): written details of how much sth. will cost 13 **tune up** (n.): act of making the motor more powerful

Act One / Scene Eleven

[At home. PAUL *set to begin housework.]*

PAUL *[Fooling]:* My! Just look at all this mess.

[He puts on record player – rock music, and dances round in time to the music while he cleans. He gets more and more foolish, and fails to notice man in doorway. The officer makes notes on almost everything.]

OFFICER: Paul Hughes?

PAUL: Yes. *[He turns off the music.]*

OFFICER: I rang, but no one answered. The door was unlocked so … School Attendance Officer, District Board of Education.

*[*PAUL *doesn't understand.]*

Truancy. You checked out of school three weeks ago. They sent me to see what's going on.

PAUL: Right now it's the housework.

OFFICER: Your mother doesn't do it?

PAUL: She works.

OFFICER: You alone all day?

PAUL: Yes. No. Well, I go down the road, see Mrs. Davidson, help her with her sewing.

OFFICER: Sewing.

PAUL: She makes things for sale. I help her.

OFFICER: You do any school work at all?

PAUL *[Doubtful]:* Yes.

OFFICER: Any math?

PAUL: I do my mother's accounts. Twice a month, I'm presenting her with a statement – what she's spent, all that. Boy, is she more careful what she spends –

OFFICER: *School* math. What school math did you do yesterday?

PAUL: Yesterday? *[Thinks.]* None.

OFFICER: Day before yesterday?

PAUL: None.

OFFICER *[Writing]:* No math done.

PAUL: Yes, I have.

OFFICER: You just said you didn't.

PAUL: You asked what I'd done yesterday and the day before so I said "none". But Monday, I did ten pages.

OFFICER: You trying to be smart?

11 **truancy:** act of staying away from school without permission

PAUL: No. *[Shows him the book.]* Ten pages ... sometimes I do more. I reckon I'm about a chapter ahead of class.

OFFICER: In some of these you don't show any working.

PAUL: I used a calculator. With problems it's not the working out, it's what to do with the numbers, isn't it?

OFFICER *[Totally unimpressed]:* Calculators aren't allowed in school.

PAUL: They are here. *[Laughs.]*

OFFICER: Geography.

PAUL: We hope to go to Mexico next year. I'm getting all the brochures –

OFFICER: Right now your class is doing Canada.

PAUL: No, no, we don't want to go to Canada.

OFFICER: What's the capital of Saskatchewan?

PAUL: I don't know.

OFFICER: Regina.

PAUL: If I wanted to know, I'd look it up in the atlas. *[Pause.]* What's the capital of Yucatan?

[No reply.]

Merida. One each. *[Laughs.]*

*[*OFFICER *walks round looking at the place.]*

OFFICER: You're breaking the law, you understand? I have to make a report. I have to report back what work you're doing, what books you're reading –

PAUL: I've just started *Foundation* ... the Asimov –

OFFICER: Not fiction! What textbooks you're reading. Show me the non-fiction books you're reading right now.

*[*PAUL *starts getting them.]*

OFFICER: And while you're about it, bring me your written work.

PAUL: Written work?

OFFICER: Social studies, history, written expression.

PAUL: I don't write it down, I just do it. *[He brings books to* OFFICER.*]*

OFFICER: How do we know what you're learning if you don't write it down?

PAUL: I wrote a lot of stuff down at school and I still don't know it. They made me write "separate" a hundred times and I still get it wrong.

OFFICER: I have to take something back with me. I've got to have something to hold up in front of the Board.

PAUL: How about me?! *[Laughs.]*

23 **"Foundation" = "The Foundation Trilogy"**: series of science fiction novels by Isaac Asimov (1920–)

[Pause while OFFICER *stares at* PAUL *with considerable dislike.]*

OFFICER: I think pretty soon you're going to find yourself in trouble.

PAUL: That's OK – I'm used to it.

OFFICER: Those the books?

PAUL: Yes.

OFFICER *[Smiles.]: The Chevy Owner's Manual* and *The Reader's Digest Guide to Sewing.*

Act One / Scene Twelve

[At home. ROBERTO *enters carrying his toolbox.]*

ROBERTO: I took her round the block – she sounds great now. Put your foot down … feel the force of G's.

PAUL: What about the brakes?

ROBERTO: Stop on a dime.

PAUL: Great, thanks. I've got your money here. *[Hands it over.]*

ROBERTO: Sure. You don't tell the tax man, that's all.

PAUL: I made some coffee. You want some?

ROBERTO: Sure. Why not?

PAUL: It's too bad you're not qualified. Couldn't you go to night school?

ROBERTO: Don't want nothing to do with no schools, night or otherwise.

PAUL *[Hesitates.]:* Would you … like me to teach you to read?

ROBERTO: Ten years at school, they don't teach me. You think you can?

PAUL: I could try.

ROBERTO: I don't want no favors.

PAUL: You'd have to pay me.

ROBERTO: Hey!

PAUL: In Spanish lessons. Here … I found an old beginning reading book … Grandma's, I guess. The words are real easy.

ROBERTO: Sure, sure, easy when you know them.

PAUL: Look, the first word's cat, see.

ROBERTO: Sure. Cat. Get me through night school, no trouble.

PAUL: Hold on. These two words are "on" and "the" … so you can use the context …

ROBERTO: Yeah, yeah.

6 **Chevy = Chevrolet:** large American car 10 **G = gravity:** fantastic acceleration 12 **on a dime:** promptly · **dime:** small American coin worth ten cents

PAUL: ... to guess the other words. So it's "the cat something on the something".

ROBERTO: Pissed on the floor.

PAUL: No, no!

ROBERTO: It's context, man!

PAUL: You weren't even trying. Can't you see they've got the same letters in them that cat has so they must sound the same –

ROBERTO: Shit, man, can't you see I don't give a rat's ass about what the cat's doing, or little kids off on picnics or apples in Farmer Jones' orchard – I don't care, see. And you getting me to guess words – word attack, huh? You think I don't know all those terms, they threw them all at me till in the end they gave up and put me in a class with all the other dummies. You want word attack? Guessing from the context ... I'll show you. *[He opens his toolbox.]* OK, you lie on the floor as if you're under the car. Go on.

*[*PAUL *does so.]*

OK, you lying there, oil's dripping in your eyes, the whole engine likely to fall on your face, and what you need is a 7/8 socket wrench – quick. OK, take it.

PAUL: Which one is it?

ROBERTO: Guess.

*[*PAUL *picks one up.]*

Uh huh, guess again.

*[*PAUL *picks up another.]*

Wrong again, come on, man, you ain't even trying, use the context.

*[*PAUL *again picks the wrong one.]*

You can do better than that, "your brother was one of the smartest kids we had in this school, now you can't even guess a simple –"

*[*PAUL *picks up another one.]*

Good boy, about time. Now, what you want it for?

PAUL: I don't know.

ROBERTO: That's right! By the time you get the word you forgotten what you were reading and couldn't care less anyway. So let's forget about me learning to read, huh. *[Walking out]* You want your car fixed again, you know where to find me, OK.

10 **orchard:** piece of land where fruit trees are cultivated 13 **dummy** (sl.): very stupid person
18 **socket wrench** (AE): Steckschlüssel

Act One / Scene Thirteen

[At home. PAUL *and* MARGIE.*]*

MARGIE: This math looks OK to me. You have any problems with it?

PAUL: No, the book explains it pretty well.

MARGIE: You seem to be doing fine there. Listen, loved your story.

PAUL: Really?

MARGIE: It's great. Did it take you long?

PAUL: Three or four days.

MARGIE: I hope you do some more. Try and get your apostrophes in the right place.

PAUL: I get confused.

MARGIE: Once there was a hospital that was trying to raise funds. And they put up this large sign saying "Help Our Nurses Home". And they left off the apostrophe.

PAUL: I don't get it.

MARGIE: It looked as though they wanted people to volunteer for escort duty. I know punctuation and grammar can be boring, but you must learn to get it right, to present your work properly. The stuff I have to set at work … people are semi-literate these days. Did you get any chemistry done?

PAUL: Couldn't.

MARGIE: Why not?

PAUL *[Pleased]:* We haven't any lab equipment.

MARGIE: Aha, well, that excuse won't hold water much longer. I've sent for a mail order catalog of chemistry equipment.

PAUL: You can't teach me chemistry.

MARGIE: We can go to night school.

PAUL *[Laughs.]:* You!

MARGIE: Just because I've never learned up till now doesn't mean I'm banned for life. I might surprise you. OK, this is it … big project coming up.

PAUL: You sound like Miss Logan.

MARGIE: Boy, you really know how to hurt a person. The trip to Mexico – I want you to plan it.

PAUL: Plan it?

MARGIE: Find out where to go, what to see, how to get there, what it'll cost.

11 **raise funds:** find money to finance sth. 18 **semi-literate:** unable to write correctly
23 **hold water** (idm.): be convincing

PAUL: We must go to Mexico City.
MARGIE: Oh yes! The museum.
PAUL: A guy at school said Mexico City has the biggest roller coaster in the world.
MARGIE: Paul! Planning the trip was supposed to be an extremely subtle way of getting you interested in the country and finding out about the Mayans and the Aztecs.
PAUL: I know. And I've started reading about the Mayans. Do you know what they did to young virgins? Sacrificed them by throwing them down a well. Not much of an incentive to stay pure, was it?

Act One / Scene Fourteen

[At BETTY'*s.]*
BETTY: You can cut these out for me – from the pattern.
PAUL: More tote bags?
BETTY: Uhuh.
PAUL: What if I make a mistake?
BETTY: Then you're in big trouble. But you won't.
PAUL: Did you ever make your living at this? Before –
BETTY: No! I was a nurse.
PAUL: A nurse!
BETTY: In the Army. I was in Vietnam.
PAUL: I didn't know you'd been to Vietnam.
BETTY: Well, I was. It was how I met Chuck ... a real corny romance.
PAUL: Was he wounded?
BETTY *[Slight pause]:* In a way.
PAUL: What was it like? Was it like MASH?
BETTY *[Sharply]:* No! Everyone thinks that – It was horrific, awful –
*[*MARGIE *enters, almost in despair, holding a letter.]*
Margie, you OK?
MARGIE: I found this ... in the mail.
PAUL: Is that the registered one? The mailman got me to sign for –
MARGIE: It's a summons. From the School Board. They're taking us to Court on a truancy charge.

3 roller coaster: Achterbahn **10 well** (n.): deep hole with water at the bottom · **incentive:** stimulus, motivation **22 corny:** melodramatic, sentimental **25 MASH** (abbr. for "Mobile Army Surgical Hospital"): satirical TV program set during the Korean War **31 summons** (pl. **summonses**): official order to appear before a lawcourt

BETTY: Well ... I suppose it was only to be expected.

MARGIE: I didn't expect it though. I thought... I don't know what I thought. *[Pause.]* Do you think what I'm doing is the wrong thing?

BETTY: It's not my business.

MARGIE: You do, don't you?

[Pause.]

BETTY: It's not what I would do –

MARGIE *[Angry]:* No, of course not, what would you know about it? What decisions do you ever have to make? Husband bringing home a fat salary, house full of gadgets, meals on the table at the right time, everything clean ... what would you know about *anything*?!

[Silence.]

[Whispers.] I'm sorry.

[Slight pause.]

BETTY: Listen, why don't you go and see them? Find out what's involved; see if there's a way out of it.

MARGIE: What's the use?

BETTY: You can't be any worse off. You've nothing to lose.

MARGIE: I might. I might go and see them in my lunch hour. Thanks. *[Getting up to go]* And what have you made for tea tonight?

PAUL: Casserole.

MARGIE: Again!! And what has that Roberto of yours done to the car? I pulled away from the lights this morning and left a Thunderbird for dead.

Act One / Scene Fifteen

BRONSKI: Mrs. Hughes, you made no secret you were keeping Paul out of school. The attendance officer wasn't satisfied with the work Paul was doing at home. Your son's been out of school for some weeks now and you've given no indication when he's likely to go back. I don't see what alternative the Board had but to prosecute.

MARGIE: You turned down the exemption without even listening to what –

BRONSKI: You have the right of appeal.

MARGIE: Nobody told me that!

BRONSKI: But your chances of winning an appeal are almost zero.

10 **gadget:** small instrument of little necessity 23 **pull away from sth.:** drive away quickly from sth. · **leave sth. for dead** (sl.): leave sth. far behind · **Thunderbird:** fast American car 28 **prosecute sb.:** take legal action against sb. 32 **appeal** (n.): act of asking a higher law court to change a decision

MARGIE: So the whole thing's a charade.

BRONSKI *[Smoothly continuing]:* One: you have a full-time job. Two: you have no college degree. Three: you're not a certified teacher.

MARGIE *[With contempt]:* A teacher! A teacher's just somebody who goes straight from school to college and back to school again so as to avoid contact with real life.

BRONSKI: Then there's Paul himself. *[Referring to the file]* Some comments at random: "Underachiever"; "argumentative"; "unco-operative reader".

MARGIE: Unco-operative what?!

BRONSKI: It's what it says here.

MARGIE *[Reaching for the file]:* Let me see that.

BRONSKI: School records of this sort are confidential, Mrs. Hughes. Official use only.

MARGIE: Good God, people have access to their FBI files if they want them! When *was* that? I know! Way back when he started school – all that reading aloud in chorus garbage. He hated that. Are those comments going to follow him round for the rest of his life?! Why don't you tattoo them on the kids' foreheads and be done with it?

BRONSKI: The point is that it seems the child has some problems which need to be ironed out by the school.

MARGIE: The point is that whatever problems he has got are caused *by* the school. Take him out of school, no problems. Miracle cure.

BRONSKI: Mrs. Hughes, I'm only trying to present things to you from the Board's viewpoint.

MARGIE: What about my viewpoint?! Doesn't anyone care about that? Why should I prove *in advance* that I can do as well as some clear-skinned little virgin? Why can't I keep him home for a few months, and then you can come and see how well he's doing?

[Pause for BRONSKI *to consider different tack, perhaps puts his arm round her.]*

BRONSKI: I know your son would get all the learning and attention from you that a child could possibly get. But do you know what the real problem is? Why the Board won't let him go? "Cause he's white and he's bright".

*[*MARGIE *tries to say something but he overrides her.]*

You know how the public measures the efficiency or otherwise of a

1 **charade** [ʃəˈrɑːd]: farce, absurdity 7 **file** (n.): collection of documents 8 **at random:** chosen in no special order · **underachiever:** (here) person who learns less than others 17 **garbage** (AE): (here) stupid idea 30 **tack:** approach 35 **override sb.:** (here) ignore sb.

school system? By the SAT scores. Every bright child they lose to the system, the average goes down just that little bit. Every white child they lose, the integration figures look just that little bit worse. The Board members are political animals, voted into office … there's no way they're going to let your son go. Especially when the Law is entirely on their side.

MARGIE: So he hasn't a chance! The Board needs him to provide some sort of statistical yeast.

BRONSKI: Mrs. Hughes, we're here to act in the best interests of the child. I don't make the rules, but it is my job to carry them out.

MARGIE: Precisely the defense used by the Nazi War Criminals. And it didn't hold water there!

BRONSKI *[Suddenly changing again]:* You know what we can do to you. Truancy charge – if they find you guilty – fined $40.

MARGIE: I'll write you a check now.

BRONSKI: Forty dollars each day out of school. You still refuse to send him to school we can take your child away from you, send him to a children's center and you to prison.

MARGIE: And this is in the best interests of the child, is it?

BRONSKI: We've done it, Mrs. Hughes. You don't believe me, check the records. *[Pause.]* Suppose you get Paul back to school … within a week, say … I think I could get the Board to drop the truancy charge. Forget the whole thing.

[Pause.]

MARGIE: Fuck you, I'm still going to appeal. I don't care if I do lose, I can still tell them what I think of them – and their lousy system.

BRONSKI: You're entitled. I'll send you the date and time to report.

Act One / Scene Sixteen

*[*MARGIE *at work.* AKERMAN *enters.]*

AKERMAN: Mrs. Hughes … talk to you a minute? Mrs. Tyler, almost quitting time, you may as well go.

[A pause while MRS. TYLER *"goes".]*

AKERMAN: Mrs. Hughes, what's wrong?

1 **SAT** (abbr.): Standard Achievement Tests 8 **yeast** [ji:st]: Hefe 26 **lousy** (infml.): stupid, useless

[No reply.]

I have here a woman who used to be punctual, cheerful, and efficient, who's now miserable and whose work is all to hell. And today! An hour and half for lunch!

MARGIE: I'm sorry. I'll get things sorted out soon, I promise.

AKERMAN: Over the years, I've found it can be a number of things; change of life, problems with husband or loved one – or both; woman next to you eating garlic. But nothing … nothing that talking about hasn't helped.

[Still she says nothing.]

Now if I were a depression boss, I'd put my feet up on the desk *[Doing the actions to suit the words]*, take out a cigar and remind you there are twelve million people out there looking for a job. So either tell me what's wrong or let me do the decent thing and fire you.

MARGIE: I've withdrawn my son from school. Because he was unhappy and not learning anything. They won't give me an exemption. I'm on a truancy charge; and if I don't send him back they can send Paul to a juvenile center and me to prison. Not one person understands why I'm doing it. And all my friends and relations treat me as if I'm some sort of freak. That's all.

[Silence.]

AKERMAN: Taken your kid out of school, huh?

MARGIE: Yes.

AKERMAN: Good for you. I wish the hell I had. *[Pause.]* Drink?

MARGIE: Sure.

[He produces bottle and pours them each a drink.]

AKERMAN: Mrs. Akerman and I have a son. Bright … interested … fun. IQ way up here. Could've been anything. At home, his room was like a museum … a laboratory. High school he got straight D's; labeled this, that, and the other. They fought him and fought him … turned him off education for ever.

MARGIE: What's he doing now?

AKERMAN: No idea. No idea where he is. *[Pause.] [Quietly angry]* You could not – even if you tried you could not – devise a stupider, more inefficient method of passing on knowledge. Thirty kids, all with different backgrounds and abilities and interests – and you try to teach them all the same thing at the same time. Something they don't

8 **garlic:** Knoblauch 17 **juvenile center:** institution for young criminals 19 **freak** (sl.): abnormal person with unusual ideas 28 **D:** low mark (the best mark is an "A") · **label sb. sth.:** classify sb. as sth. 29 **they:** (here) the school 33 **devise sth.:** invent sth., think sth. up

particularly want to learn anyway … Madness! Madness! How's your son liking it? How's he handling it?

Margie: He found it tough at first – couldn't handle the freedom. Even now, I'm not sure how much actual school work he's doing, but he's certainly learning. He handles my money, he's learning to fix the car, he's planning a trip for us –

Akerman: That's it, that's it! Because he *wants* to learn those things. All the other junk school teaches he'll find out when he needs to. If he ever does. So … they've come the heavy on you, have they? Truancy … prison threat?

Margie: The lot.

Akerman: Full-time job, out all day, therefore uncaring mother.

Margie: I've no other choice. I need the money and I'm damned if I'm going on welfare.

Akerman: They turned you down – is that an end to it?

Margie: I can appeal. But I've no chance. They made that very clear. I'm about ready to forget it all … send him back to school.

Akerman: No, no, no! That's the weapon of bureaucrats – make you give up before you start to fight. Always, always force them to make the decision, make them accountable, make them live with it. If you withdraw now, they've won.

Margie *[Defeated]:* I know.

Akerman: Those guys never have to risk a thing. They never have to put their money, their ass, even their job on the line. You can't let them get away with it. Let's have a go at them.

Margie: How?

Akerman: I don't know – we'll think of something.

Margie: What's this "we", Mr. Akerman?

Akerman: You enjoy fighting this all by yourself?

Margie: No.

Akerman: OK, then. And I've just thought of something. To help. As of now, I'm firing you.

[End of Act One.]

8 **junk** (infml.): useless things 9 **come the heavy on sb.** (infml.): threaten sb. 20 **make sb. accountable:** make sb. take the responsibility

Act Two / Scene One

[At home. Music playing. Paul *and* Grandmother *playing chess.* Margie *returns, with* Gordon. *All except* Gordon *have drinks.]*

Margie *[Announcing]:* Gordon. Dropping in again unannounced. It's getting to be a habit.

Paul: Twice in seven years.

Margie: We are having cozy pre-prandial drinks afore the Sunday dinner. Have a drink.

Gordon: Thank you. I'd appreciate it if I could talk to you for a –

Margie: Do. Talk to me. Go ahead. You have before you an aural sponge.

Gordon: Alone.

Margie: No, no, no … only leads to acrimony. We're having a little celebration – a month since I left work.

Paul: Since you were fired.

Gordon: Fired?

Margie: Only technically. Dear Mr. Akerman fired me because he was then obliged to pay me a month's wages and I was free to apply for welfare. Which, mercifully, I don't have to do because I have found me some part-time employment. Paul's been working extremely hard – lots of schoolwork if you want to see it.

Paul: Like me to square a root?

Margie: Furthermore your son is now a passable cook. Not passable in the exam sense, of course, but …

Paul: Like an omelette?

Margie: Even grandmother is slowly coming round to our point of view.

Grandmother: I have to admit Paul is doing a lot more school work at home than I thought he would.

Margie: And she is fulfilling her familial role. Takes Paul on outings of an educational nature.

Grandmother: I've been showing him the city. Its history.

Margie: Its history-see! You have before you a potential Renaissance man. In short, Gordon, things are going swimmingly … you have nothing to worry about. And how are things with you? Tell us what's new in pustules.

[Pause.]

6 **cozy** (AE) = (BE) **cosy:** intimate · **pre-prandial** [ˌpriːˈprændɪəl] (humorous or fml.): before lunch · **afore** (humorous or old use): before 9 **aural:** related to the ear · **sponge:** Schwamm 11 **acrimony** [ˈækrɪmənɪ]: bitterness and anger 31 **swimmingly** (infml.) (adv.): (here) joyfully and easily 33 **pustule** [ˈpʌstʃuːl; BE -juːl]: Eiterpickel

Gordon: I would still like to see you alone –

Margie *[Remembering to tell him]:* Done some research! Found out a lot. Some very impressive arguments to put before the Board. At the appeal. Next month.

Gordon: Listen to me! In the first place I don't want my son to be some sort of educational hippie. Taking him out of school, you're taking him out of his society … you're making him an outsider. In the second place – and far more important – he has to go to school if he's to get his high school diploma, and he has to have that to take college entrance exams, to get a degree, to get into grad school –

Margie: That's all an education means to you, isn't it? – acquiring diplomas and qualifications.

Gordon: Well, it is! And he can't get anywhere without a high school diploma.

Margie: Which he can get without going to school.

*[*Gordon *silenced by this.]*

Margie: Research!!! He can get high school equivalence – night classes, second chance classes. And you don't have to be attending school to sit college entrance exams.

Gordon: If he doesn't go to school, he'll never get a job!

Margie: But if he does, he will? Twelve million unemployed – they all went to school.

[Pause.]

Gordon: What happens if you lose the appeal – he goes to school, right?

Margie: Wrong. We move to another state. If he's not enrolled in a school, the authorities'll never catch up with us. Win or lose, he stays out.

Gordon: Except I'm going for custody.

[Silence.]

I've been to see a lawyer – I have a good case.

Margie: You'd take Paul away from me.

Gordon: Yes.

Margie: You'd do that.

Gordon: If they turn down the exemption, it's because Paul's not getting an adequate education. And that's a good enough reason to take him away – crossing the state line won't do you any good then.

Paul: I'd have to come and live with you.

Gordon: I'd be doing it for your own good, Paul.

10 **grad school** = **graduate school:** university 16 **night class:** class attended in the evening after work 17 **second chance class:** class attended by people who did not finish their schooling 24 **enroll sb. into sth.:** register sb. for sth. 25 **catch up with sb.:** find sb. 26 **custody:** right of taking care of sb. (esp. a child)

Act Two / Scene Two

[At BETTY*'s.]*

PAUL: Don't tell her I told you.

BETTY: Of course I won't.

PAUL: He'll probably send me to boarding school.

BETTY: Well … a lot of people like boarding school.

PAUL: I wouldn't.

BETTY: I can't see them taking you away from your mother. Not after all these years. Truly.

*[*PAUL *remains gloomy.* BETTY *gives him an envelope.]*

BETTY: Here. Towards Mexico.

PAUL: What …

BETTY: It's your pay.

PAUL: You don't have to –

BETTY: I know. But you've helped me a lot. It's only fair.

PAUL: Great. Thanks a lot.

BETTY: How's the paper route?

PAUL: OK. I'm getting quicker now I know the route. I had to collect the money last Saturday – I got quite a few tips.

BETTY: Perhaps I should do it.

PAUL: You could! They need more people. They always have vacancies as soon as the cold weather hits. I'd help you.

BETTY: No, thank you.

PAUL: Want me to sew up these tote bags? No charge.

BETTY: No, that lot's for the workshop.

PAUL: What workshop?

BETTY: I take them to the Retarded Citizen's Workshop. They finish them off … it's something they can manage, and then the shop sells them to raise funds.

PAUL: You mean this sewing I thought I was so smart doing, retards can do!

BETTY *[Sharply]:* Some people are retarded. They are *never* "retards"!

PAUL: Sorry.

BETTY: I hate hearing them called that.

PAUL: Sorry. How often do you go there?

BETTY: Twice a week.

26 **retarded** [rɪˈtɑːrdəd]: mentally handicapped 29 **retard** [ˈriːtɑːrd] (derog. sl.): sb who is mentally handicapped

Paul: Isn't it pretty creepy?

Betty: Paul, it's not madmen in straight jackets lunging at you. They're very nice, most of them. And they love having visitors.

Paul: But aren't they … mad?

Betty: No! They're, well, not able to cope with everything; they need help – protection. I'll take you along some time.

Paul: No, thanks.

Betty: Even Dean and Brian have survived a visit.

Paul: I'll think about it.

Betty: Here, try your hand at sewing up these coveralls.

Paul: Can they do these at the workshop?

Betty: You'll just have to come along and find out for yourself, won't you?

Act Two / Scene Three

[At home. Margie *at table, telephone book open, making phone calls.]*

Margie: Mrs. Abbott? Congratulations, you have just won a gift worth many dollars. I'm part of a research team that is doing a survey in this area to find out how many homes have installed a security system. Can you tell me if you have a system in your home? You haven't? Well, our company is prepared to install one of their wonderful systems in your home entirely free for a period of one month which would normally cost you – you wouldn't? Quite understand, thank you for giving me so much of your time.

[She ticks off name and dials next number.]

Margie: Mr. Abel? Congratulations, you have just won a gift worth many dollars. I'm part of … hallo? *[Rings off.]* No fooling Mr. Abel. *[Dials again.]* Mr. Abelman? No? I must have dialed a wrong number, I'm sorry. No matter. This is your lucky day, you have just won a gift worth – is it what?!!? Do I like to what … ?!! You filthy pervert!! *[Slams down phone.]* The answer is "yes", I do like it. *[Checks book, stops, then rings number.]* Mr. Akerman? Congratulations, you have just won a gift worth many dollars – a phone call from Margie Hughes. Yes! Just thought I'd call … see how things were … Great! And work? … All systems secure? Just checking, oh, we're fine, fine … everything going really well. Paul's working hard … got a newspaper route and I've got this sales job and my

1 **creepy:** frightening 2 **straight jacket:** Zwangsjacke · **lunge at sb./sth.:** move suddenly forward to attack sb./sth. 10 **coverall:** one-piece, protective working clothes

husband's suing for custody and this job is probably the most demeaning job in the world – he'll sue if I lose the appeal, which I will, they told me, and I'm giving up this job right now, I've decided this very minute. I haven't got a chance with the appeal, I can't lose Paul, I can't, not to anyone, especially not to Gordon, of all people, that would be unbearable, I couldn't face it, Christ, whose child is it, I put time and energy and thought and care and love and they talk about taking him away, I'd kill for him. You know that, I'd kill for him… *[She stops as she listens to what* AKERMAN *is saying.]* … Oh, oh would you?… here would be … No. You're wrong, I can talk to almost anyone; you're the only person I can listen to.

Act Two / Scene Four

[Outside. PAUL *is rolling newspapers and putting elastic bands around them. He then puts them in a delivery bag.]*

PAUL: Come on, Ma.

*[*MARGIE *enters wrapped up but shivering.]*

MARGIE: Oooooooooooooooooohhhhhhhhhhhhhhhh.

PAUL: I've done most of yours.

MARGIE: Oooooooohhhhhhh. It must be ten below.

PAUL: It was twelve below yesterday. Here. *[He gives her a loaded bag to sling over her shoulder. Helps her on with it.]* You do that side of the street, I'll do this. Got your list?

MARGIE: Yes. *[She can bearly hold it for shivering.]*

*[*PAUL *throws a paper expertly.* MARGIE *throws one. Hopeless.* PAUL *retrieves it and throws it properly.* MARGIE *throws another. Almost as bad.]*

MARGIE: This is hopeless. I'll never get the hang of it.

PAUL: You think this is tough you wait till you start trying to get people to pay their accounts.

MARGIE: Oh God… *[She throws another, still feeble. Recovers it and places it in the right place.]*

PAUL: Think of the hundred and twenty dollars, Ma.

MARGIE *[With contempt]*: Huh! *[She throws the next one, this time it's perfect.]* I did it, I did it!! Paul, I did it!!

PAUL: Nice throw, Ma. Wrong house, but nice throw.

1 **sue** [su:] **sb.:** take sb. to court · **demeaning:** lowering one's self-respect; humiliating 15 **shiver** (v.): shake with cold 18 **ten below:** 10° Celsius below zero 24 **retrieve sth.:** get sth. back 25 **get the hang of sth.:** learn how to do sth. 28 **feeble:** weak

Act Two / Scene Five

[ROBERTO and PAUL together. On another part of the stage MARGIE is pacing up and down preparing her appeal to the board. She has notes in her hand.]

ROBERTO *[Holding up paper]:* That's what I want to learn to read.

PAUL: "Application for driver's license. Sample questions."

ROBERTO: Eighty questions, man. Each with different answers.

PAUL: Multiple choice.

ROBERTO: They pick twenny of them – you got to get fifteen right.

MARGIE: "Ladies and gentlemen of the Board…" No. "Board members…" Mr. Chairman. By saying that my son must remain in school, you are saying that he cannot be educated outside it. Let me give you some facts. It is a fact that we acquire most of our knowledge outside of school. It is a fact that a child can miss the first seven years of school and make it all up with a few months of good teaching. It is a fact that in England adults who want to learn French can learn in three months what it takes children eight years in school.

PAUL: "How close to a fire hydrant may you park a motor vehicle? a) five feet, b) six feet, c) ten feet?

ROBERTO: Ten feet. Hell, I know all the answers. It's the questions I don't know.

PAUL: Are there *any* words you recognize in the question?

ROBERTO: What if I do? I ain't going to be able to learn eighty questions. Never.

MARGIE: There is no evidence whatsoever that students taught by certified teachers do better than those taught by uncertified teachers.

PAUL: This word … see … is "hydrant".

ROBERTO: Sure … hydrant.

PAUL: Look at it. There's only one question in the eighty that has hydrant in it. If you recognize hydrant then you know what the whole question is.

ROBERTO *[Slowly accepting the idea]:* Yeah.

PAUL: You won't need to know the rest of the words. And you know the answer, "C". So if you learn "Hydrant – C", that's all you need. Can you remember which one was hydrant?

5 **sample question:** example or test question

*[*ROBERTO *points.]*
Yes.

MARGIE: The compulsory education laws were introduced not to force children to be in certain buildings for a certain number of hours a day, but to ensure they got an education. I am just as keen as you are that he gets an education – but you are saying that what I am doing is a criminal act.

PAUL: Here it says "U-turn", OK?

ROBERTO *[Finding it]:* "U-turn".

PAUL: Answer, "B".

ROBERTO: "U-turn – B". That's all I can take today, man.

PAUL: OK. Can you help me with my Spanish now?

ROBERTO: Sure.

PAUL: Qué es la población de España?

ROBERTO: Ay! Qué machito cabezudo! Those Mexicans hear your accent, they're gonna double their prices. All this stuff out of a book – no good to anybody, man. You want to speak Spanish come around to our house – nobody speaks nothing but.

MARGIE: If schools claim to guarantee an education – how come this country has 23 million illiterates?

Act Two / Scene Six

[Outside. PAUL *and* GRANDMA *walking.]*

PAUL: Is this place safe?

GRANDMA: I want to show you something.

PAUL: Grandma, this is a ghetto.

GRANDMA: It's round the next corner.

PAUL: I haven't seen a white face for ten minutes.

GRANDMA: You've nothing against blacks, have you?

PAUL: It's what they might have against me. Why are we coming here?

GRANDMA: You'll see. *[To herself]* Corner store …

PAUL: Let me take you away from all this.

*[*GRANDMA *stops.]*

GRANDMA: This is it.

PAUL: What?

8 **U-turn:** Wende

GRANDMA: The house I was brought up in.
PAUL: Here!!! This house!
GRANDMA: Certainly was. Looks smaller everytime I see it.
PAUL: Cute. Let's go.
GRANDMA: It's all right. That was my room, see, right at the top. I wonder if they'd mind if we went in and –
PAUL: No!
GRANDMA: No, it'd be a mistake.
PAUL: Do you remember any of these people?
GRANDMA *[Laughs.]:* When I was a little girl, this was a well-to-do white area. Course, it was one family to a house then.
PAUL: You had the whole house to yourselves?
GRANDMA: We did. Soon after I left, the area began to change … it became Italian. Fifteen, twenty years ago it started to change to black.
PAUL: What next?
GRANDMA: Wouldn't surprise me if the white middle classes didn't discover it all over again. Funny, when you're little you think things'll always be the same … and you're brought up on the assumption that the world will be the same when you're grown up as it is now. And it never is … everything changes.
PAUL: Can we go now?
GRANDMA *[Sees something on the sidewalk.]:* Ah … not everything. *[She does a few hops of hopscotch.]*

Act Two / Scene Seven

*[*AKERMAN *makes a phone call.]*
AKERMAN: Mr. Bronski, please …
*[*BRONSKI *answers his phone.]*
BRONSKI: Bronski.
AKERMAN: Mr. Bronski? And how's the wonderful world of bureaucracy this morning? Sitting comfortably?
BRONSKI: Er –
AKERMAN: My name's Akerman. I'm calling on behalf of Mrs. Hughes whom you doubtless recall … withdrew her son from –
BRONSKI: Yes.

4 **cute:** nice 19 **assumption:** unquestioned belief 24 **hopscotch:** (Spiel) Himmel und Hölle

AKERMAN: The appeal against the decision not to grant an exemption.

BRONSKI: Yes.

AKERMAN: Just thought you should know how things stand in the event the appeal is turned down – she tells me you kindly pointed out this was likely to be the case. If that occurs then I think we would all find ourselves in court. On opposing sides.

BRONSKI: Yes, once the appeal's rejected the Board is taking Mrs. Hughes to court on trua–

AKERMAN: No, Mrs. Hughes would be taking the Board to court.

BRONSKI: The Board! On what grounds?

AKERMAN: Constitutional. She would be fighting your right to compel the boy to attend school.

BRONSKI: State law provides for compulsory schooling.

AKERMAN: *Schooling* is compulsory. But the state system has no right to an educational monopoly. In other words, schooling can take place other than at a public school. The legal precedents being Michigan vs Nobel; Perchemlides vs Frizzle –

BRONSKI: I am aware of them.

AKERMAN: Furthermore the onus would no longer be on Mrs. Hughes to prove that Paul is getting an adequate education, but for you to prove that he isn't. A very different matter. I believe State of Iowa vs Sessions covers the point –

BRONSKI: I am aware of that case also. In short, you are threatening us.

AKERMAN: A threat! A threat!!! Nothing was further from my mind. But I know it can help to be fully aware of all the implications before making a decision.

BRONSKI: Thank you. I've taken a note of your comments –

AKERMAN: Just one more thing. This picture keeps running through my mind: Mrs. Hughes, solo parent, making financial and other sacrifices, standing on the court steps being filmed by TV cameramen on her fight against bureaucracy. And the news going into all the homes – that people have the right to educate their children at home.

BRONSKI *[Smiles.]:* You're grossly over-simplifying the issue.

AKERMAN: Of course!! As will the television news.

[Pause.]

BRONSKI: What was your name again?

11 **compel sb. to do sth.** [- ˈ-]: force 16 **precedent** [ˈpresɪdənt]: earlier decision by a law court regarded as an example 16–17 **Michigan vs Nobel, Perchemlides vs Frizzle:** real legal cases 19 **onus** [ˈəʊnəs]: responsibility

AKERMAN: Akerman.
BRONSKI: Of?
AKERMAN: Akerman Printing.
BRONSKI: Printing! I thought you were a lawyer.
AKERMAN: Now did I say that? Goodbye. *[Rings off triumphant.]*

Act Two / Scene Eight

[Lights up on MARGIE *reading aloud.]*
MARGIE: "'... What faces will smile on me when I die!' cried his companion shivering. 'Who will talk to me in those long nights! They cannot come from home; they would frighten me, if they did, for I don't know what it is, and I shouldn't know them. Pain and fear, pain and fear for me, alive or dead. No hope, no hope!'
The bell rang to bed: and the boy, subsiding at the sound into his usual listless state, crept away as if anxious to avoid notice. It was with a heavy heart that Nicholas soon afterwards – no, not retired; there was no retirement there – followed – to his dirty and crowded dormitory."
PAUL: Gee, I'm glad there aren't any places like Dotheboys Hall nowadays.
MARGIE: Of course there are, Paul. Only now they're called summer camps. Hey, I want you to know you're doing a good job with the house, the cooking, all that. I appreciate it. In fact, bought you a present.
PAUL: A present!
MARGIE: Don't take it too seriously.
PAUL *[Seeing shape]:* Wow, it's not even a book. *[Opens it.]* A tie.
MARGIE: You recognized what it was. Well done.
PAUL: What do I want a tie for?
MARGIE: To look your best. For the appeal ... to make an impression on the Board.
PAUL: Oh sure ... they're gunna say ... "Kid's math is lousy but didja see his tie!!", "Kid got a tie like that, must be doing OK."
MARGIE: You have to look your best.
PAUL: In this? What a design! Yuk!!
MARGIE: That was very expensive.
PAUL: I could do better. I can't even tie a tie.

12 **subside:** sink 13 **listless:** without energy or enthusiasm · **anxious:** eager 14 **retire:** withdraw; go to bed 15 **dormitory:** large bedroom containing many beds 16 **Dotheboys Hall** ['du:ðəbɔɪs]: boarding school to which Nicholas Nickleby was sent as an assistant in Charles Dickens's novel *Nicholas Nickleby*

MARGIE: Come here … come on … come here.

PAUL *[In mock terror]:* Oh my God, not the tie … I'll tell you anything you want, but not the tie …! *[*PAUL *snatches the tie from her.]* This is what guys from school use a tie for.

[He starts flicking her with it, driving her back from him. She grabs it off him and they start wrestling. PAUL *screams.]*

It's a snake. It got me, it got me. *[He does a dying act, head in her lap.]*

MARGIE: Yippee! No more casserole.

Act Two / Scene Nine

[Chairman of the Board's visit.]

HARRIS: Mrs. Hughes, good of you to see me. *[He puts brief case on table.]* I've been Chairman of the Board number of years, I've found more things can be settled out of the Board room than in it. *[He takes sandwiches out of brief case, starts eating them.]* Excuse me, only time I've got today. Now, I was wondering if there were other ways of solving this … different school perhaps, we can waive the zoning bit, or a special class or find you a really special teacher, one who could handle your son, know what I mean?

MARGIE: That's not the issue –

HARRIS: See, I hate to think we've failed him in some way; I'd feel badly about that. I'd like you to give us one more chance. Schools take a real beating these days. Parents questioning methods, challenging what's taught, hauling teachers off to court the minute they lay a finger on their offspring. There's no discipline 'cos there's no respect. Same time society's always hollering at us to do something about drugs or racism or drunken driving – any social ill, school's supposed to find the answer. Plus provide enough space engineers – or whatever. You know we feed more than half the kids in our district – breakfast and lunch. Half of those we have to take care of after school. Health – we have to see to that, too. Won't be too long before we're expected to let them sleep over as well. I had very little time to give to my kids – too busy setting up the business. *[Hands her a card.]* Catering. Supply two airlines here, three hotels, got our own cafeterias … I said to my kids, you listen to the

15 **waive sth.:** make an exception regarding sth. · **the zoning bit:** (hier) Gesetz, der das Einzugsgebiet betrifft 20–21 **take a beating:** be under attack 22 **haul sb. off to sth.:** make sb. appear before sth. 23 **offspring** (pl. **offspring**)(infml.): child(ren) 24 **holler at sb.:** criticize sb. in a loud voice 29 **sleep over:** spend the night

teacher, do what the teacher tells you ... best advice I ever gave. *[Takes out photo.]* Gary, in engineering school; Michael is a pharmacist for the hospital; Ken, not too sure what he wants right now, but majoring in physics this year. And little Mary ... she would have to be the best nursing sister you ever saw. They all, all of them went through the public school system. Right here, in this district. They came from an ordinary home, hell, I didn't get through high school. What about kids from the ghetto? School's the place that introduces them to the world of books, music, art ... some cases it's a refuge from violence.

Margie: All I want is to get –

Harris: Scuse me. You see, get an exemption you got to prove he's getting equivalent education at home. Pretty hard to do. So it should be. Free, universal education ... it's a noble concept, if you think about it. Countries that haven't got it, doing their damnedest to get it. But parents start taking kids away – it's bad enough them going to private schools, but you start taking them away to teach them at home, the system's going to crumble. Now we're not going to be browbeaten, we'll hear you out, but I'm proud of this district, the schools in it, they're doing better each year, and we're not going to lie down dead all for one call from your Mr. Akerman. Pleasure talking to you, Mrs. Hughes. *[He puts sandwich back in briefcase and goes.]*

Act Two / Scene Ten

[At Betty*'s.* Paul *and* Betty *enter.]*

Betty: Well?

Paul: Well, what?

Betty: You didn't say a word in the car ... about what you thought about the workshop.

Paul: I made a complete idiot of myself.

Betty: No, you didn't.

Paul: I didn't know what to say to them ... I couldn't talk to them ... not properly. That boy making the stuffed toys –

Betty: Thomas.

Paul: I asked him if he could play chess. How could I have been so stupid? He must have thought I was trying to make fun of him. And someone

3 **major in sth.:** study sth. as a main subject 11 **scuse me** (non-standard pron.): excuse me 14 **do one's damnest** (infml.): try very hard 17 **browbeat sb.** [braʊ'biːt]: frighten sb. 18 **hear sb. out:** listen to everything sb. wants to say 30 **stuffed toy:** toy filled with soft material

else I was telling about computers and then I suddenly stopped thinking, hell, he won't understand this, and then I got embarrassed that he'd know I'd stopped because I thought that.

BETTY: I know they enjoyed your coming to see them.

PAUL: Then they must be even stupider than I thought! *[Groans.]* No ... you know what I mean ... how could they have enjoyed me ... I didn't know what to say. I just mumbled. That man in the T-shirt and shorts –

BETTY: Jamie.

PAUL: He asked me what sort of doors we had in our apartment. I didn't know. He wanted to know if they had panels, and how many panels and whether they were rectangular or square, what type of handles, how many hinges, were the door frames grooved ... I didn't know, I couldn't remember. I felt an idiot.

*[*BETTY *smiles.]*

It felt like they knew it all and I knew nothing.

Act Two / Scene Eleven

[Alternates from MARGIE *and* AKERMAN *to* ROBERTO *and* PAUL. AKERMAN *and* MARGIE *are walking at night.]*

MARGIE: That was a wonderful meal. Thank you.

AKERMAN: Pleasure.

MARGIE: All you've done for me, I should have paid for you.

AKERMAN: Listen, I still give up my seat to ladies in the subway.

MARGIE: Do you really?

AKERMAN: Well, I did in 1956. You buy someone else a meal sometime.

MARGIE: Stop being avuncular.

AKERMAN: My role in life.

[Pause.]

MARGIE: Mrs. Akerman know where you are?

AKERMAN: Remember bridge night and keep it holy.

MARGIE: Why do you always refer to her as Mrs. Akerman?

AKERMAN: Oh, that's just a little nickname I have for her. Her real name is Mrs. Akerman.

MARGIE: Can we sit here for a bit? Watch the river.

AKERMAN: Why not?

10 **panel:** part of a wall, door or ceiling made of wood 12 **hinge:** Türangel · **grooved:** having grooves (= Rillen) 24 **avuncular** [əˈvʌŋkjələ; BE -jʊl-]: like a kind, friendly old uncle 28 **bridge:** card game

MARGIE: Don't be too eager. How often do you get asked to sit in the moonlight with a young—ish woman?

AKERMAN: Happens all the time.

MARGIE: Fool.

[At ROBERTO*'s.* PAUL *and* ROBERTO *going over driving test.* PAUL *is correcting answers.]*

PAUL: Sixty-four. That's good.

ROBERTO: Not if the ones I got wrong all turn up in the test.

PAUL: One or two might … but not all of them. Anyway, go over the ones you got wrong. Try this one again.

ROBERTO *[Finds a word.]:* "School" … so it's the school bus … gotta stop ten feet behind it when it's stopped. "B".

PAUL: "School" is right. But it's asking about the speed limit in a school zone …

ROBERTO: 15 mph. "A".

PAUL: Right. So if you see a question with school in it, you've got to find one more word. "Zone" 's easy – not too many words start with Z. "School" and no z …?

ROBERTO: Ten feet … "B".

MARGIE: There is something romantic, isn't there? About big ships going to sea? *[She suddenly imitates a ship's siren.]* Wouldn't you like to sail round the world in a yacht?

AKERMAN: No.

MARGIE: No, nor would I. Tell me your favorite sin.

AKERMAN: That hardly fits my avuncular role.

MARGIE: No, go on, go on.

AKERMAN: All right. Take a beautiful afternoon … the sun warm and inviting … birds singing … everything in nature beckoning you to enjoy the outdoors … and you draw the curtains firmly, select a good book and get into bed.

MARGIE: You dirty beast. You're a wicked uncle.

[Pause.]

AKERMAN: About Thursday night.

MARGIE: Oh, oh, oh, oh – this was the first night I hadn't thought about that appeal for weeks. I even dream about it, you know that.

AKERMAN: Sorry.

28 **beckon sb.:** signal with the hand that sb. should come to you

MARGIE: What! Say it! You've mentioned it now.

AKERMAN: It's… nothing. What were you thinking of wearing? On Thursday?

MARGIE: Oh, the silver G-string, matching navel jewel and a tassel on each nipple.

AKERMAN: That's all right then.

MARGIE: What is the point you were going to make?

AKERMAN: In a way you're going to be on trial. I mean if you were charged with being a prostitute it would be unwise to show up in court wearing a slit skirt, and a tight blouse.

MARGIE: That was the alternative I had in mind.

AKERMAN: Wear what they want you to be, not as what they think you are.

MARGIE: And what's that?

AKERMAN: A freak.

PAUL: A couple more days, you'll be ready.

ROBERTO: You think I should make an appointment? For the test.

PAUL: If your driving's OK.

ROBERTO: My driving is great.

PAUL: Go ahead. We'll make sure you know these last ones by then.

ROBERTO: All these parking ones … park here, don't park here. *[He is pointing them out.]* See, it's everywhere.

*[*PAUL *stares at him.]*

PAUL: You know something? I never showed you "park".

ROBERTO: So?

PAUL: So you read that all by yourself.

[Smile from ROBERTO *as he realizes.]*

ROBERTO *[Excitedly]:* Hey … Dad …!!!

AKERMAN: So you take in the textbooks you're using, the samples of Paul's work, the note you've prep–

MARGIE: Yes!

[Pause.]

AKERMAN: Sorry, I brought up the subject.

MARGIE *[Angry]:* It's OK.

[Pause. She suddenly clings to him. It leads to a kiss.]

4 **G-string:** Minislip · **navel** [neɪvl]: Nabel · **tassel:** Troddel 5 **nipple:** Brustwarze 10 **slit skirt:** skirt with a long narrow opening at the side exposing much of the leg 32 **bring sth. up:** begin to talk about sth.

MARGIE: I thought you were never going to do that.
AKERMAN: So did I.
MARGIE: A sin?
AKERMAN: No.
MARGIE: Can we go home now?
AKERMAN: Sure.
[They stand. She waits to be embraced again.]
I'm sorry.
MARGIE: Sorry?
AKERMAN: I mean, this is it.
MARGIE: I thought … I thought …
AKERMAN: I was doing all this to …
MARGIE: Yes.
AKERMAN: Avuncular, remember. Let's get you home.

Act Two / Scene Twelve

[At McDonald's.]
GORDON: This OK?
PAUL: It's OK.
GORDON: I thought every kid liked McDonald's.
PAUL: Every *kid* does.
GORDON: Sorry. *[Pause.]* I wanted you to know why I've come down to speak at the appeal tomorrow.
PAUL: Because you want me back in school.
GORDON: You look on me as some sort of whistle-blowing-everybody-out-of-the-pool spoilsport, don't you?
PAUL: I guess so.
GORDON: I felt the same about my Dad. He kept saying, "One day you'll be grateful".
PAUL: And one day you were.
GORDON: Yes, I was.
PAUL: It doesn't follow that I will.
GORDON: I've seen so many guys mess up their lives. Drop out at school or college and they all think it won't matter or they'll get back in … and it doesn't happen. They end up in a dead-end routine job … they're stuck … they're no longer free to choose. *[Urgent]* I've seen it happen, Paul!

24 **spoilsport:** person who stops others enjoying themselves

It's not funny... *[Sees he's still not making impression.]* I don't know why I bother.

PAUL: You never have in the past.

GORDON. Meaning?

PAUL: Once you left you never took much interest.

GORDON: I stayed away on purpose! Deliberately. My God, I wanted to see you. But I've seen what it does to people – adults and kids – to have one parent visiting every now and then, a million visits to the zoo, meals in places like this. Outings and treats. The one who has them is seen as a cruel disciplinarian; the one who visits, a weekend Father Christmas. I vowed I'd never do that.

PAUL: Is all this trying to tell me I can't have a hot fudge sundae?

GORDON: Do you know why I left your mother?

PAUL: For a younger woman?

GORDON: I left because your mother has never been able to cope with reality.

PAUL: You tried living in our apartment?

GORDON: Margerie sees everything through books. *[This does catch* PAUL*'s attention.]* It's more than escape ... it's not that books are life, life is books. She believes in the printed word. She wants advice, she goes to a book. She wants to learn something, she uses a book. She'd always rather consult a book than a person. That trip round Europe nearly drove me crazy. It wasn't just that we had to go where the guide books said, but Keats sat here, and Byron screwed here, there and everywhere else. Half the time she tried to see things as if she were a Henry James heroine. Or in Venice: she kept looking out for a beautiful boy in a sailor suit!!

PAUL: I don't get that.

GORDON: I'm pleased to hear it.

[Pause.]

PAUL: Why a skin specialist?

GORDON: What?

PAUL: It's kinda feeble, isn't it? Hardly life and death.

GORDON: Oh well ... specialist because you want patients who are sick only in office hours. Skin? ... It's the most fascinating organ of the lot.

2 **bother** (v.): trouble oneself 11 **vow** [vaʊ] (v.): make a solemn promise 12 **fudge sundae:** dish made from ice-cream fruit, nuts, etc. 24 **John Keats** (1795–1821), **Lord Byron** (1788–1824): famous English Romantic poets · **screw** (v.) (infml.): have sex 25 **Henry James** (1843–1916): American-born novelist 26–27 **a beautiful boy in a sailor suit:** reference to Thomas Mann's *Death in Venice*

Tell you what, you come to Boston some time, I'll take you round the hospital, show you what I do. Then we'll go home and I'll play you my collection of skin flicks.

*[*PAUL*'s eyes widen.]*

PAUL: Skin flicks!!!

GORDON: Sure.

PAUL: Skin flicks – you mean … *[Realizes he's been had.]* Argggghhhhh, I get it … dermatology films.

GORDON *[Kidding]:* Of course, what other kinds are there?

[They both laugh.]

Act Two / Scene Thirteen

*[*MARGIE *is alone. Perhaps in the dark. Listening to music.* PAUL *switches on light. Surprised to see her there.]*

PAUL: Sorry.

MARGIE: That's all right.

PAUL: You OK?

MARGIE: Yes. You have a good time with Gordon?

PAUL: Sure. Scared about tomorrow?

MARGIE: Scared. About whether I'm doing the right thing. Am I?

PAUL: I don't know.

MARGIE: That's not very comforting.

PAUL: Well, I don't, do I? How can you tell?

[Silence.]

MARGIE: Don't say to me I'm a bad parent.

PAUL: You do OK.

[She opens her arms for a hug. He sits by her and she holds him. Reaches for Nicholas Nickleby *and begins to read.]*

PAUL: I think, actually, I'd rather read the rest of it to myself. *[After a moment, he releases himself from her gently.]* Good night.

[She is left alone. She gives a cry of despair.]

3 skin flicks (sl.): play on words: 1) dermatology films, 2) pornographic films **25 hug:** sign of affection by putting one's arms around sb.

Act Two / Scene Fourteen

[In the Board Room, BRONSKI *is placing papers for the board members in waiting area. Outside,* GORDON *arrives and sits down.* JULIA BEYER *arrives in Board Room, looks at the papers.]*

JULIA: I don't see the text book complaint on the agenda.

BRONSKI: Waiting for the committee's report.

JULIA: Good. Longer they delay it, the better. Lot of nonsense.

*[*BRONSKI, SEDILLO *and* KRAMER *enter together.]*

KRAMER: I'm on the tenth green in one … one! Up till now, haven't had one six on my card … evening, Julia.

JULIA: Evening.

KRAMER: I'm forty feet from the pin, but I figure, go for it, I've shots in hand – oh-oh, excuse me.

[He hurries out. JULIA *looks inquiringly at* SEDILLO.*]*

SEDILLO: Stomach bug – he told me all about it before he got onto golf. In even greater detail.

*[*MARGIE *and* PAUL *arrive and sit in waiting area.* MARGIE *is holding books and papers.]*

SEDILLO: Are you letting us away early tonight?

BRONSKI: Immunization policy for new admissions; three zoning appeals; summer school schedules.

SEDILLO: Real exciting.

BRONSKI: First there's an exemption appeal.

*[*AKERMAN *arrives in waiting area, to* MARGIE*'s surprise.]*

AKERMAN: I never can resist a dramatic ending.

*[*MARGIE *doesn't reply.]*

And I thought you'd need moral support.

MARGIE: But it has to be moral.

[Chairman hurries in, with paper cup of coffee.]

HARRIS: Evening, evening, evening, are we ready to start? *[He goes straight to his place, ready to begin almost immediately.]* Can we begin?

*[*KRAMER *returns, explains to* HARRIS.*]*

KRAMER: … Stomach upset … if you see me slipping out …

4 **agenda:** list of things to be discussed at a meeting 8 **be on the green:** hit the golf ball onto the green with one long drive 9 **a six:** (here) act of putting a golf ball in the hole in six shots 11 **pin:** flagpole in the hole on a green 11–12 **in hand:** below the necessary number 14 **stomach bug:** minor stomach illness

HARRIS: Sure, Pete, quite understand. First up is … appeal of Mrs. Hughes against decision not to grant an exemption. Frank.

BRONSKI: The background papers are in front of you. The situation is that we turned down her request for her son, Paul, to be exempt from attending Glenn Junior High so that she can teach him at home. She appealed against that decision and that's what we are hearing tonight. No medical or religious factors involved; legally the law is entirely on our side. What we have to decide tonight is whether there are any special circumstances that we didn't take into account when we made the original decision, and whether these circumstances are such that they warrant it being changed.

HARRIS: I should add that she has talked of taking us to court should we turn down the appeal, and would challenge us on constitutional grounds. Frank thinks she could have a chance there. I wanted you to know this, but it shouldn't be considered in reaching our decision.

JULIA: Not going to be blackmailed into it.

HARRIS: Exactly. Do we see her right away.?

BRONSKI: The boy's father, Dr. Hughes – he and Mrs. Hughes are divorced – wanted to address the Board; I said that was in order.

[The Board nod agreement.]

AKERMAN: You'll be fine … just keep calm.

BRONSKI *[In waiting area]:* Dr. Hughes.

AKERMAN: They're just a bunch of laymen … you know as much as they do.

BRONSKI *[To the Board]:* This is Dr. Hughes … the boy's father.

GORDON: Thank you. May I say, Mr. Chairman, how much I appreciate the opportunity you've given me in addressing the Board tonight. I know my former wife is going to ask you for my … our son to be exempt from school so that she can teach him herself. I know the reasons for her wishing to do this, but in my opinion, the disadvantages far outweigh the advantages. My main concern is for his future. 1. How can she provide the expertise of that supplied by a high school staff, each of whom has a degree in whatever subject they teach, when she has no college degree at all? 2. Were he eventually to obtain high school equivalence, which I doubt under present circumstances, what college of any standing would accept him? 3. I'm a professional person. I don't necessarily want Paul to follow in my footsteps but I want him to be *able* to do so if he chooses. Any professional school requires the highest qualifications for

11 **warrant sth.** ['wɔːrənt; BE 'wɒ-] (v.): justify sth. 16 **blackmail sb.:** force sb. to do sth. by threatening him or her 23 **bunch** (infml.): group · **layman:** non-expert 37 **professional school:** training school for a certain profession

admission; God knows the competition was tough enough in my day; it's even more difficult nowadays. Mr. Chairman, my wife is gambling with my son's future … and with each day he is kept out of school, the odds against increase.

HARRIS: Yes. Thank you. Anyone wish to comment?

KRAMER: Can't fault all that.

*[*SEDILLO *nods in agreement.]*

JULIA: Trying to decide what is likely to happen in the future is speculation – whether Paul is at school or not.

GORDON: The speculation is based on what he's doing at present.

JULIA: Well, what is he doing?

BRONSKI: This is what the Attendance Officer had to say: "Irregular work habits. Insufficient means of instruction in the home. Disregard of current curriculum goals and school objectives. No written evidence of work supplied. Insubordinate attitude."

KRAMER: Can't see how she can argue against that.

JULIA: But she is entitled to. Argue against it.

BRONSKI: Which is why we're going through all this.

HARRIS *[Dismissing* GORDON*]:* Thank you.

GORDON: Thank you. There's no objection if I stay?

HARRIS: It's an open meeting.

[He nods to BRONSKI *to fetch* MARGIE*. The Committee relaxes for a moment. Talking among themselves. When* BRONSKI *enters,* AKERMAN *signals to* MARGIE *to stay calm. He goes on in ahead. She remains a while longer, bracing herself for her entrance.]*

HARRIS *[To* AKERMAN*]:* Er …?

AKERMAN: Akerman.

HARRIS: What's your position in relation to –

AKERMAN *[Smiles.]:* Coach.

[He sits. MARGIE *storms into the meeting.]*

MARGIE: Right! Sit down!

[Reaction.]

I don't want to hear any talking. Sit down. *[To* BRONSKI*]* You, too!

HARRIS: Mrs. Hughes.

MARGIE: When I said sit down and stop talking it applied to every single person in this room. Right. This –

HARRIS: Mrs. Hughes.

3–4 **the odds against increase:** the chances of sth. happening become worse 6 **fault sth.:** find a mistake in sth. 13 **disregard of sth.:** no attention paid to sth. 14 **current:** present · **goal:** aim; objective 15 **insubordinate:** unwilling to obey 19 **dismiss sb.:** tell sb. he or she may leave

MARGIE: This lesson –

BRONSKI: The procedure for a hearing is –

MARGIE: You'll get your turn later, in the meantime sit down and keep quiet. This lesson was supposed to start on the hour –

KRAMER: We're not here for a lesson!

MARGIE *[Overriding him]:* – and it is now four minutes past, so we are late!

BRONSKI: This is a formal meeting and the Chairman has –

MARGIE: I'm prepared to stay here all night if that's what it takes.

HARRIS: Mrs. Hughes.

MARGIE: Right!! Spanish. Pass these along. *[She hands papers to* HARRIS.*]* Pass them out.

HARRIS *[Trying to be patient]:* I don't see what this has to do with –

MARGIE: You said you'd hear me out.

[A pause while HARRIS *remembers, yes, that's what he did say. Then he passes out the papers, and the Board members, now that their Chairman is apparently going along with it, decide to do what's requested.]*

MARGIE: Today. The difference between the two words for "to be": *estar* and *ser*. *Estar* has to do with place, where something is. *[To* BRONSKI*]* Are you paying attention? There's going to be a test at the end of this. So we say, *Miguel está en Nueva York*, Miguel is in New York. *Pero no es de Nueva York*, but he is not from New York. Where do you think you're going?

*[*KRAMER *has begun creeping out.]*

KRAMER: To the bathroom.

MARGIE: No, you don't. You sit right there.

KRAMER: But I have an upset stomach!

MARGIE: Did you bring a note?

KRAMER: Course I didn't bring a note.

MARGIE: Well, you sit right down there and get on with your work. *Miguel está enfermo*, Miguel is sick; *pero él no va al escuso*, but he is not going to the john.

*[*JULIA *is now thoroughly enjoying this.]*

On your sheets you'll find the present tense of both verbs. We'll say them out loud together.

[Faint mumbles of resentment.]

It's the way to learn them! *[She begins and slowly they join in.] Ser* to start with. *Soy, eres, es ... somos, sois, son*. Terrible. Again.

31 **john** (AE sl.): toilet 35 **resentment:** feeling of bitterness or anger

[This time they are a bit louder.]

Soy, eres, es … somos, sois, son. And now *estar: estoy, estás, está … estamos, estáis, están*, yes?

*[*SEDILLO *has his hand up.]*

SEDILLO: Shouldn't you point out that *ser* also refers to something permanent – such as a characteristic or an occupation.

MARGIE: I see – we have a know-it-all in our midst. That's covered in the next lesson.

SEDILLO: I happen to be a native speaker of Spanish.

MARGIE: It won't do you any harm to go over it again. *[To them all]* Come on – I want those work sheets finished.

[Some of them filling in the work sheets. Somebody's ink has run out and they are trying to borrow another. KRAMER *flings down his pen.]*

KRAMER: I'm not going to do this, this is ridiculous. It's not as if I'm even interested in Spanish …

MARGIE: Not interested in Spanish! May one ask why not, pray?

KRAMER: Because I had it up to here with Spanish in school!

[Pause.]

HARRIS: I think we've spent enough time on this.

MARGIE: Yes. Agreed. Put away your books, hand up those work sheets. Come on, hurry it up.

[General air of relief at lesson being over.]

Right – math! *[She starts handing out another set of sheets.]* Quadratic equations. Numbers one through eighteen.

[This time they take no notice of what she is asking them to do. A pause.]

HARRIS: Mrs. Hughes – what was the point of all that?

MARGIE: You said the only way for me to get an exemption was for me to provide equivalent education. You think I can't provide the equivalent of that?

BRONSKI: We're busy people, Mrs. Hughes – we haven't got time to play games.

MARGIE *[Screaming]:* Games! You threaten me with prison, with taking my son away. You call that games! You talk about the best interests of children. You have no idea. Schools destroy kids, don't you understand? They destroy them. And you force me, force everyone to send their children. *[Sobbing.]* You lousy, stinking hypocritical bastards. What right … what right have you to do this? *[She has almost collapsed.*

7 **know-it-all:** person who knows everything and shows off his or her knowledge in an unpleasant way 16 **pray** (old use or sarcastic): please 24 **equation:** mathematische Gleichung 36 **sob:** cry bitterly · **hypocritical:** thinking one thing but saying another

AKERMAN *helps her out.* PAUL *looks up in some alarm as she returns to her place, and sits crying.]*

AKERMAN: Well … you did it your way.

PAUL: Ma …?

HARRIS: Well … does much more need be said?

KRAMER: What a lulu! Boy, get him back to school just to keep her away from him a few hours a day.

JULIA: Couldn't you see what she was trying to do! The stupid, mindless teaching methods –

SEDILLO: Oh-oh, Julia's launching into a speech –

JULIA: I say let's grant her the exemption.

KRAMER: You crazy?

HARRIS: That's a no vote, Pete?

KRAMER: You bet.

*[*HARRIS *looks at* BRONSKI.*]*

BRONSKI: Absolutely not.

*[*HARRIS *looks at* SEDILLO. SEDILLO *pauses a moment, then shakes head.]*

[In the waiting area.]

AKERMAN *[Getting up to go]:* Come on … no point in waiting.

*[*PAUL *removes his tie. They help* MARGIE *to her feet.]*

HARRIS: So, three against –

GORDON: Mr. Chairman … shouldn't you see my son?

HARRIS: See him? I thought you wanted us to turn down the appeal.

GORDON: The issue is about him. Isn't it? Surely she deserves … the issue deserves … a bit better hearing than you're giving it.

BRONSKI: The officer saw the boy.

JULIA: Hear, hear. I want to see him. *[To the others]* Aren't you even curious? A mother like that … what she has produced.

SEDILLO: I think we should see the boy.

HARRIS: I've no objection. You're right, we'll see him.

*[*BRONSKI *has to go to get* PAUL. *He catches them just as they're leaving.]*

BRONSKI: Paul Hughes – see you now.

*[*PAUL *starts trying to tie his tie as he goes in.]*

PAUL: I was supposed to wear a tie. *[He struggles with it.]* Shoot, she bought it specially.

HARRIS: It doesn't matter about the tie.

6 **lulu** (sl.): lunatic 10 **launch into sth.:** start doing sth. with enthusiasm 14 **you bet** (AE infml.): you are right; I agree 34 **shoot:** polite way of saying "shit"

JULIA: Here.

[She helps him with the tie.]

HARRIS: Julia ...

JULIA: You can still ask him questions. You can speak, can't you?

PAUL *[Slightly strangled]:* Yes.

KRAMER: Julia, forget the goddamned tie.

HARRIS *[Attempting to keep meeting going]:* Paul ...

JULIA: You tie it then.

HARRIS: Paul, you've been away from school for some time; are there any things that you miss about it?

PAUL: The computer. Programming is real neat.

KRAMER: So that's one thing straight away you can't get at home.

PAUL: I'm going to get one of my own – I'm earning enough to get one.

JULIA: There. *[She tucks his shirt in as well.]*

SEDILLO: What would your feelings be if you were told you had to go back to school tomorrow?

PAUL: Kinda frustrated I guess. I mean, I'm just sort of organized now. Earning and learning. Hey, just thought of that, sounds good.

HARRIS: The thing that concerns the Board, Paul, is what the school attendance officer had to say.

PAUL: The who?

BRONSKI: Truancy officer.

PAUL: Oh boy, what a weirdo. Like something out of the Gestapo.

HARRIS: He said you weren't doing enough work.

PAUL: He didn't listen to a thing I said. I tried to tell him all the things I was doing.

SEDILLO: Well, tell us.

PAUL: It sounds kinda feeble –

SEDILLO *[Kindly]:* Go on.

PAUL: Car maintenance ... handling a bank account and arranging a loan.

KRAMER: You don't need to know those things yet.

PAUL: I haven't needed quadratic equations either.

SEDILLO: Anything else?

[Pause.]

PAUL: Sewing.

KRAMER: Sewing!

PAUL: I can make a lot of things on the sewing machine ...

11 **real neat** (AE infml.): really great 23 **weirdo** (sl.): strange person

JULIA: Bravo.

KRAMER: Sewing!!

PAUL: Sell you a neat tote bag for five bucks. Make a great Christmas present. Only joking. It's really interesting … I've never made things before.

JULIA: Tell us what you think is the most interesting thing you've done since you left school.

PAUL *[Thinks.]:* Collecting the newspaper money. There are some amazing people on my route – a guy who used to run a naval shipyard, a woman who danced with …

BRONSKI: All this is irrelevant! The key point is, you're not keeping up with your school work. At home. Are you?

PAUL: I bet I'm way ahead in science and math. And Spanish.

BRONSKI: But behind in most other things?

*[*PAUL *doesn't reply.]*

SEDILLO: Paul, tell me one thing. Are you convinced your mother is doing the right thing?

PAUL: No.

KRAMER: See! Even the kid thinks she's wrong.

PAUL: I didn't say that. I'm not completely convinced she's right … on the whole I think she is. I mean it wouldn't break my heart if I had to go back to school.

JULIA: But would it hers?

PAUL: Pretty near. I don't see why it's such a big deal, what she's doing. Why are you all making such a big fuss over it?

BRONSKI: Because it's against the law!

PAUL: But it wouldn't be if you gave us the exemption. *[Pause.]* Why don't you pretend I'm ill … "Allergic to chalk dust" or something. I know you have to work your butt off to get into college. I'm not stupid. I'm not going to let myself get too far behind in things I need. And if I need to go back to school, I will. Any time. All you are saying is you don't trust me. Or Ma. Why don't you just leave us alone to get on with it?

HARRIS *[Dismissing* PAUL*]:* Thank you.

*[*PAUL *goes.]*

[Anxious to speed things along] Any further debate. No. All those in favor of granting an exemption?

*[*JULIA*'s hand goes up immediately. A slight pause, and* SEDILLO*'s hand goes up.]*

3 **buck** (AE infml.): dollar 9 **run sth.:** be in charge of sth. · **naval:** Marine- · **shipyard:** Schiffswerft 29 **work one's butt off** (infml.): work extremely hard

HARRIS: Against.

[BRONSKI and KRAMER against.]

Chairman has casting vote. I vote in favor of the exemption. Item two on the agenda, Immunization policy for new entrants …

Act Two / Scene Fifteen

[Board members depart, leaving MARGIE, PAUL, AKERMAN, GORDON *on stage.* GRANDMOTHER *and* ROBERTO *join them, as does* BETTY.*]*

AKERMAN: You did it!

MARGIE: We won, we won, we won, …

PAUL: I did it.

GRANDMOTHER *[To audience]:* A pyrrhic victory?

BETTY: Congratulations … You're free … no more worries.

[Gradually they start speaking more to us.]

MARGIE: We went to Mexico … stayed three months in the end. No job, so no reason to return any sooner.

PAUL: Ahora, sé hablar muy bien español.

ROBERTO: Hey! *[Holds up driver's license, proud of the license and of the fact he can read the words.]* "License to drive a motor vehicle …"

MARGIE: And when we got back, it was how I thought it would be.

PAUL: I zoomed ahead in math and science.

GRANDMOTHER: Lagged behind in everything else.

GORDON: I bought Paul a computer. It was something I could do.

BETTY: He still came to see me … though not as often. He lost interest in the sewing … only natural, I suppose. I used to try and compare him with Dean … his work. It seemed to me he was keeping up … but without the battles. And he knows a lot more than Dean … about life.

MARGIE: It's great!!! He works hard at whatever interests him, then moves on to something else. It's the natural way. And we take off on trips when we feel like it … we earn a bit of money when we can. It'll work out. I'm sure of it.

GRANDMA *[Dismissive]:* Ach, what the hell, I've given up worrying. School or no school, college or no college, he's going to be what he's going to be.

GORDON: He's been up to Boston a few times. I've shown him round the

3 **casting vote:** last vote to decide an issue when votes on each side are equal 10 **pyrrhic** [ˈpɪrɪk]: victory that is worthless because the winner suffers great losses 20 **lag behind:** not do as well as others

hospital, shown him what I do. He seemed really interested. He's a great kid. I'm still hoping he'll make it to college, maybe to med school. He's got the brains.

AKERMAN: Why can't we trust kids more? Give them more credit? Every kid comes into this world wanting to learn … but by the time they're grown we've killed that desire in almost every one of them.

[By now, only PAUL *and* MARGIE *are left on stage in the light.]*

PAUL: Boy, they're all waiting, holding their breath – will I or won't I go to college? You can tell … that's the test … success or failure or The Great Experiment. The answer to everything. I'll get there … in my own time … and when I've decided what I want. I'm going to make another trip first … heading off on my own.

[He goes, leaving MARGIE *alone.]*

MARGIE: And so they go … and there's nothing more you can do about it and you're left to look backwards. Asking all the futile questions: should I have …? What if I'd …? If only … The swimmer in the cold sea turns to wave from time to time, but you're alone … as you always were … But taking Paul out of school was the best thing I ever did for him. It was. The best thing. You have to believe that.

[End.]

2 **med:** medical 12 **head off** (v.): start off 15 **futile**['fju:taɪl]: useless

A Multiple Choice Test on *Multiple Choice*

A multiple choice test offers options from which the right one has to be chosen. There is always *one* correct answer among the possibilities offered, but please remember that in some cases, more than one answer can be correct. Be careful: there are usually one or two items (so-called "distractors") which only serve to distract you from the right choice (i.e. the key).

1. Roger Hall was born
   ❍ a) in New Zealand.
   ❍ b) in Australia.
   ❍ c) in England.
   ❍ d) in the U.S.A.

2. The expression *Down Under* refers to
   ❍ a) Australia and New Zealand.
   ❍ b) New Zealand.
   ❍ c) Australia.
   ❍ d) neither Australia nor New Zealand.

3. Paul's favourite subjects are
   ❍ a) science and mathematics.
   ❍ b) physical education and mathematics.
   ❍ c) Spanish and physical education.
   ❍ d) domestic science and geography.

4. Paul's father Gordon is
   ❍ a) a skin specialist.
   ❍ b) a dentist.
   ❍ c) a psychiatrist.
   ❍ d) a dermatologist.

5. Margie works
   ❍ a) for a successful publisher.
   ❍ b) for a printing firm.
   ❍ c) for Mr Akerman.
   ❍ d) at home. She is a housewife.

6. The capital of Yucatan is
   ❍ a) Regina.
   ❍ b) San Cristobal.
   ❍ c) Merida.
   ❍ d) Mexico City.

7. Margie and her husband Gordon separated because
   ❍ a) he fell in love with a younger woman.
   ❍ b) she betrayed him with another man.
   ❍ c) Gordon could not live with Margie's sense of reality.
   ❍ d) Margie was a bad housewife and mother.

8. When Paul and Roberto met, Roberto was
   ❍ a) a handicapped person.
   ❍ b) a weird lulu.
   ❍ c) a retarded person.
   ❍ d) illiterate.

9. At the end of the play, Paul
   ❍ a) decides to go back to school.
   ❍ b) is determined to go to college and later to med school.
   ❍ c) does not exactly know what is going to happen to him.
   ❍ d) turns into a social drop-out.

In examinations, these multiple choice tests are evaluated, mainly by computers, according to a point system. Sometimes, wrong answers are subtracted from the right ones, which means that it is not always wise to make a cross at random and rely on the chance that it happens to be in the right place.

Solutions: 1. c; 2. a; 3. a; 4. a, d; 5. b, c; 6. c; 7. c; 8. d; 9. c

Listening to the Author

How did I learn to become a writer?

It was a long and slow progression. I always "wanted" to be a writer, and had had a story published in a national children's magazine when I was 14, but after that wrote nothing for several years. The idea of being a writer appealed, but not the work.

I began writing regularly when I left home to go to New Zealand by myself at the age of 19. I wrote numerous letters home to my parents and friends, averaging three or four letters a week which I consider the first step in my apprenticeship. I was also keen to be a film critic, and so I would write a review in an exercise book of every film I saw. (None of these were ever published.) I also wrote a few short stories.

My first published writing was an article I wrote about my experiences as a waiter, but it was when I started at teachers' college and university (attending both concurrently) at the age of 23 that I began to write a great deal, mostly for the college magazine: stories, humorous articles, poetry, book and film reviews. I was also doing a great deal of acting, in particular for stage revues where I used to write and perform my own material. After seven years of this, I was invited (well, I asked and they accepted) to write and act on television in a comedy series.

But in between I had been sending material to all sorts of places: to the *New Yorker*, to *Punch*, to New Zealand magazines, all of whom sent my work back, and soon I had an impressive collection of rejection slips. I wrote a brilliant script for a television comedy series set in England. The only problem was that no one else thought it was brilliant. I sent in material to radio in New Zealand – and heard nothing back from them. Of course, I was discouraged, but never so discouraged that I gave up.

One thing that kept me going was fantasising about success. My definition of success then was to be interviewed on television. I *longed* to be interviewed on television: I knew I would come across as handsome, witty and modest. My favourite variation of this fantasy was that I would be a success in the UK, fly back to NZ, do my witty TV interview. *Then* (we're getting close now) that night there would be a gentle knock on my hotel room door and there would be a woman (in some versions several

5 **appeal** (v.): be attractive 8 **average sth.:** einen Durchschnitt von etw. erreichen 9 **apprenticeship:** time spent learning how to do sth. from more experienced people 14 **concurrently:** at the same time 22 **rejection slip:** short standard letter to say sth. has not been accepted 26 **discourage sb.:** take away sb.'s hope or confidence 28 **long to be sth./for sth.:** want sth. very much 30 **witty:** humorous

women) who had previously spurned me, who would enter my room with a look of admiration combined with a longing, and within minutes she would be removing her clothes ... Well, not a very admirable fantasy, I admit but I mention it because often you do need some sort of psychological carrot to keep you determined (just as we all think of what we'll do *after* we have sat our exams). The only danger is if the fantasising prevents the writing.

If I am asked for advice about "how to become a writer", I can only relate what worked for me. I wrote in all sorts of styles for some years before I discovered I was a playwright, and this discovery came only when I realised that when I read novels I often skipped the prose and raced on to the next chunk of dialogue, and that when I started to write prose I very often found the pages filled with dialogue.

If you're going to write, then write. Never wait until "you feel like it", until you are "inspired", it doesn't work like that. Sit down and write. The first ten to twenty minutes are always the hardest, and then your writing will start to flow (it's like warming-up at sport).

You have to put in the hours. If you want to write, you will find the time. (I get fed up with people who corner me at parties and suggest that they, too, could do what I have done if only they "had the time", or that the whole thing is some sort of trick.) Writing is sheer hard work, and re-writing is even harder.

I have to say that I refused to let rejection put me off, I did persevere, and was always sending something away to publishers, magazines or broadcasters. The worst moment was when a lady from the BBC TV drama department cast her eyes over a script I had submitted and gently advised me that perhaps it would be best if I gave up. Twelve months later (I was now 35) my first stage play was a smash hit throughout New Zealand.

1 **spurn sb.:** turn one's back on sb. 5 **carrot** (fig.): reward promised to sb. to persuade him or her to do sth. 11 **skip sth.:** leave sth. out when reading 12 **chunk:** piece 19 **get fed up with sb./sth.:** have enough of sb./sth. 23 **persevere:** continue even if it is difficult

Questioning the Author

Before discussing *Multiple Choice* with students in a German secondary school, the editor (ARG) of this school edition discussed the following questions with the author of the play (RH):

ARG: *What prompted you to write the play?*

RH: I took a year's leave from my position at university in order to go travelling, mostly in the USA. To do this, I took my own two children (Pip, 10 and Simon, 8) out of school in order to go travelling round the USA. In fact they had about eight months out of school, then went to a public school in Washington, D.C. for one term (they were two of the very few white children in what was predominantly a black school), and then they had a term at school in New Mexico (with a majority of Hispanic children).
Taking them out of school made me think about the issue, and I read a book by the late John Holt (an educational writer whose books I admired) called *Teach your Own* which made it sound an exciting and worthwhile thing to do. Also, as Guest Artist at New Mexico State University I *had* to write a play – this was the topic that interested me at the time.

ARG: *Is the play based on your own experience?*

RH: Partly, but also on a lot of reading and talking to a few people who had done that.

ARG: *Did you write the play for anyone in particular or for a particular occasion?*

RH: I was expected to write a play for the drama students at New Mexico State University as a condition of being Guest Artist – my play was performed during my last couple of weeks there.

ARG: *Could you comment on the structure of the play as a whole, e.g. division into two acts, different length of the scenes?*

RH: I've possibly used the term "Acts" loosely. It is a play of scenes rather than two acts – the interval is simply there as an interval rather than the division into acts in the more traditional sense of the word.

ARG: *Have you seen any productions which varied greatly from your original idea or misinterpreted your intentions?*

RH: For one production in New Zealand, the director told me in advance that the set would be that of a three-ring-circus and that every character would be dressed in clown costume – the reason given by the director was that in her opinion the current Minister of

Education was “a clown”. I disagreed strongly with this approach and said so and tried to get it changed – the play is a debate play and I feared that such a setting would distract from the issues being discussed. Under the terms of a contract, a writer has to be consulted about any changes made to the *script* and since they were not going to change any of the lines, I had no legal way of preventing the production. It went ahead as the director wished. I was so unhappy with the result that I publically disowned the production and refused to accept the royalties and gave them away to a couple of charities.

ARG: *Which production of the play has impressed you most? Pleased you most?*

RH: The original production done by the drama students at New Mexico State University. I think they felt closer to the theme than any other cast that did the play subsequently. Also Marjorie Atlas, the director, spent many hours with me going over the script while it was in progress (which I didn't always enjoy) but it did mean she was very much emotionally involved with the play.

ARG: *Have there ever been any strong reactions for or against the play from audiences, critics, fellow playwrights, own family, friends?*

RH: In fact, this is one of the least produced of my plays, though it has had productions in the USA, and England as well as New Zealand. The USA setting was a problem for English and New Zealand audiences because they couldn't identify with it as much as if it had been set in their own country.

Some directors dislike it because it is a “message play”, and I have to agree this is partly true and that sometimes the message gets in the way. But most people have enjoyed it and found it stimulating, and they all seem to argue about the points the play raises. So being a “message play” may be its weakness but it is also its strength.

ARG: *Your play draws from your own experience because you agreed to your children staying away from school for almost one year. What effect, in your opinion, did this have on them? What do your children think of this year off? Are there any differences in their final assessment and in yours? Would you “do it all again”? – And would they?*

3 **distract from sth.:** draw attention away from sth. 8 **disown sb./sth.:** say that one does not want to have any connection with sb./sth. 9 **royalty:** money paid to an author or to the holder of a patent 10 **charity:** society for helping the needy 18 **be involved with sth.:** be concerned with sth. 31 **draw from sth.:** take from sth. 34 **assessment:** judgment

RH: You can't measure this, but I'm convinced it was a huge plus in all our lives, and have never regretted it. (One thing that struck us as we travelled was the number of people we met and when we told them what we were doing said wistfully "We should have done that!" So, if circumstances permit you to do this, go!!!!).
As a family it drew us even closer, and it is still a great shared experience which we still draw on. They learnt a lot, met a lot of people, learnt to be part of a minority, saw a lot of places (part of that year included four months in England so from there we went to Crete, and we also went from Las Cruces, New Mexico, to Mexico), discovered new foods … in short all the benefits of travel, but with the bonus it lasted such a long time.
Neither of them has regretted it at all, and have always regarded it as a great experience.

We *are* doing it all again. As I write this, we are coming to the end of a year in London. They are now 20 and 18. At the end of 1991, Pip had had a couple of years at university, and Simon had just finished school. Simon said he didn't want to go straight to university, and Pip was happy enough to have a year away from her studies. I was prepared to pay their air fares, and for them to share the flat we rented in London – I pointed out this was the last time I would subsidise their travels in this way.
It has been harder for them this time in that they missed their friends much more, and both play basketball at quite a high level (Pip for Otago, and Simon being selected for the national selection at his age level) and they had to give this up. Here, in London, they have worked in restaurants – Pip in a wine bar/restaurant, and Simon as a kitchen hand before he got a job as a coffee boy, then waiter. Neither of these jobs are likely to have much direct influence on their future careers, but it is all experience (I speak as a former waiter – you learn so much about people, working with them and for them). Pip rediscovered theatre, Shakespeare in particular, having been to some great productions at the Royal Shakespeare Company (but she's been to rock shows, too). Simon's been to a lot more rock shows than theatre. They both travelled round Europe on Eurorail passes and covered a lot of ground.

4 **wistful:** with unsatisfied desire 7 **draw on sth.:** use sth. as a source 22 **subsidise sb./sth.:** partly finance sb./sth.

I have to say that they would have got a lot more out of their year if they had not been with us, having to find their own accommodation, and learning to budget more and generally being a lot more independent. However, the reality was that this was a chance I offered them (since I was taking leave again and coming to the United Kingdom to write for British television) and I am sure they will return to Europe independently within a few years. And they are both returning to New Zealand independently: Pip going on safari in Africa and then home via South Africa; Simon staying on for a few weeks after we leave, and spending some time in the USA on the way back. But once again, it has been a great year, and we realise that we have been very lucky.

The Hall Family in 1982

3 **budget** (v.): plan how to spend money carefully

For Further Reading

"Let's forget this and wallow in Dickens", Margie suggests to Paul in Act One, Scene Seven. Now – what exactly is this novel, *Nicholas Nickleby* by Charles Dickens, about? Here is a summary of its contents, followed by two excerpts from the novel itself (taken from Chapters III and VIII respectively).

Summary of *Nicholas Nickleby*

Nicholas Nickleby, a novel by Dickens, published 1838–9.

Nicholas, a generous, high-spirited lad of nineteen, his mother, and his gentle sister Kate are left penniless on the death of his father. They appeal for assistance to his uncle, Ralph Nickleby, a griping usurer, of whom Nicholas at once makes an enemy by his independent bearing. He is sent as usher to Dotheboys Hall, where Wackford Squeers starves and maltreats forty urchins under pretence of education. His special cruelty is expended on Smike, a half-witted lad left on his hands and employed as a drudge. Nicholas, infuriated by what he witnesses, thrashes Squeers and escapes with Smike, who becomes his devoted friend. For a time he supports himself and Smike as an actor in the provincial company of Vincent Crummles; he then enters the service of the brothers Cheeryble, whose benevolence and good humour spread happiness around them. Meanwhile Kate, apprenticed to Madame Mantalini, dressmaker, is by her uncle's designs exposed to the gross insults of Sir Mulberry Hawk, one of his associates. From this persecution she is released by Nicholas, who breaks Sir Mulberry's head and makes a home for his mother and sister. Nicholas himself falls in love with Madeline Bray, the support of a selfish father and the object of a conspiracy of Ralph Nickleby and another revolting old usurer, Gride, to marry her to the latter. Ralph, whose hatred for Nicholas has been intensified by the failure of his plans, knowing Nicholas's affection for Smike, conspires to remove the latter from him; his plots are thwarted with the help of Newman Noggs, his eccentric clerk,

8 **generous:** ready to give more than necessary 10 **gripe:** complain · **usurer** ['juːʒərə]: Wucherer 11 **bearing:** behaviour 12 **usher** (old use): teacher 13 **urchin** (old use): small, dirty, untidy child · **under pretence of sth.:** unter dem Vorwand von etw. 14 **half-witted:** stupid; uneducated 15 **drudge:** person employed to do dirty work · **infuriate sb.:** make angry; fill with fury or rage · **thrash sb.:** beat sb. 19 **benevolence** [-'---]: quality of being good and generous 21 **gross** [grəʊs]: very strong and crude 22 **persecution:** state of being threatened and treated cruelly 25 **conspiracy** [-'--]: secret plans made by a group of people to do damage to sb. else 26 **revolting:** disgusting 29 **thwart sth.:** prevent sth. from happening

but nevertheless Smike falls a victim to consumption, and eventually dies in the arms of Nicholas. Confronted with ruin and exposure, and finally shattered by the discovery that Smike was his own son, Ralph hangs himself. Nicholas, befriended by the Cheerybles, marries Madeline, and Kate marries the Cheerybles' nephew, Frank. Squeers is transported, and Gride is murdered.

(from: Margaret Drabble (ed.), *The Oxford Companion to English Literature*, Oxford University Press, Oxford, 1985)

Excerpt from Chapter III

"Are you willing to work, sir?" he inquired, frowning on his nephew.

"Of course I am," replied Nicholas haughtily.

"Then see here, sir," said his uncle. "This caught my eye this morning, and you may thank your stars for it."

With this exordium, Mr. Ralph Nickleby took a newspaper from his pocket, and after unfolding it, and looking for a short time among the advertisements, read as follows:

"'EDUCATION. – At Mr. Wackford Squeers's Academy, Dotheboys Hall, at the delightful village of Dotheboys, near Greta Bridge in Yorkshire, Youth are boarded, clothed, booked, furnished with pocket-money, provided with all necessaries, instructed in all languages living and dead, mathematics, orthography, geometry, astronomy, trigonometry, the use of the globes, algebra, single stick (if required), writing, arithmetic, fortification, and every other branch of classical literature. Terms, twenty guineas per annum. No extras, no vacations, and diet unparalleled. Mr. Squeers is in town, and attends daily, from one till four, at the Saracen's Head, Snow Hill. N.B. An able assistant wanted. Annual salary £5. A Master of Arts would be preferred.'

"There!" said Ralph, folding the paper again. "Let him get that situation, and his fortune is made."

"But he is not a Master of Arts," said Mrs. Nickleby.

1 **consumption:** Schwindsucht 2 **exposure:** state of having all one's mistakes and wrong-doings disclosed to the public 3 **shatter:** destroy sb. emotionally 10 **inquire:** ask for information about sth. · **frown on sb.:** look with disapproval at sb. 11 **haughty:** arrogant 14 **exordium:** beginning, introduction 19 **board** (v.): provide rooms and meals for pupils 22 **single stick:** wooden stick used for fencing (= Fechten) 23 **fortification:** strengthening; making stronger 24 **diet:** food · **unparalleled:** having no equal

"That," replied Ralph, "that, I think, can be got over."

"But the salary is so small, and it is such a long way off, uncle!" faltered Kate.

"Hush, Kate my dear," interposed Mrs. Nickleby; "your uncle must know best."

"I say," repeated Ralph, tartly, "let him get that situation, and his fortune is made. If he don't like that, let him get one for himself. Without friends, money, recommendation, or knowledge of business of any kind, let him find honest employment in London which will keep him in shoe leather, and I'll give him a thousand pounds. At least,' said Mr. Ralph Nickleby, checking himself, 'I would if I had it."

Excerpt from Chapter VIII

He could not but observe how silent and sad the boys all seemed to be. There was none of the noise and clamour of a school-room; none of its boisterous play, or hearty mirth. The children sat crouching and shivering together, and seemed to lack the spirit to move about. The only pupil who evinced the slightest tendency towards locomotion or playfulness was Master Squeers, and as his chief amusement was to tread upon the other boys' toes in his new boots, his flow of spirits was rather disagreeable than otherwise.

After some half-hour's delay, Mr. Squeers reappeared, and the boys took their places and their books, of which latter commodity the average might be about one to eight learners. A few minutes having elapsed, during which Mr. Squeers looked very profound, as if he had a perfect apprehension of what was inside all the books, and could say every word of their contents by heart if he only chose to take the trouble, that gentleman called up the first class.

Obedient to this summons there ranged themselves in front of the schoolmaster's desk, half-a-dozen scarecrows, out at knees and elbows, one of whom placed a torn and filthy book beneath his learned eye.

"This is the first class in English spelling and philosophy, Nickleby," said Squeers beckoning Nicholas to stand beside him. "We'll get up a Latin one, and hand that over to you. Now, then, where's the first boy?"

13 **clamour** ['klæmə]: loud confused noise or shout · **boisterous:** noisy and violent 14 **mirth:** happiness · **crouch** [kraʊtʃ]: sit close to the ground, with arms around legs 15 **evince sth.:** show sth. 16 **locomotion:** movement 20 **commodity:** useful thing 21 **elapse:** pass, go by 22 **apprehension:** (here) understanding 26 **obedient:** doing what one is told to do · **summons:** command to do sth. or to appear somewhere 27 **scarecrow** ['skeəkrəʊ]: figure of a man dressed in old clothes, put in fields to scare away birds

"Please, sir, he's cleaning the back parlour window," said the temporary head of the philosophical class.

"So he is, to be sure," rejoined Squeers. "We go upon the practical mode of teaching, Nickleby; the regular education system. C-l-e-a-n, clean, verb active, to make bright, to scour. W-i-n, win, d-e-r, der, winder, a casement. When the boy knows this out of the book, he goes and does it. It's just the same principle as the use of the globes. Where's the second boy?"

"Please, sir, he's weeding the garden," replied a small voice.

"To be sure," said Squeers, by no means disconcerted. "So he is. B-o-t, bot, t-i-n, tin, bottin, n-e-y, ney, bottinney, noun substantive, a knowledge of plants. When he has learned that bottinney means a knowlege of plants, he goes and knows 'em. That's our system, Nickleby; what do you think of it?"

"It's a very useful one, at any rate," answered Nicholas.

"I believe you," rejoined Squeers, not remarking the emphasis of his usher. "Third boy, what's a horse?"

"A beast, sir," replied the boy.

"So it is," said Squeers. "Ain't it, Nickleby?"

"I believe there is no doubt of that, sir," answered Nicholas.

"Of course there isn't," said Squeers. "A horse is a quadruped, and quadruped's Latin for beast, as every body that's gone through the grammar knows, or else where's the use of having grammars at all?"

"Where, indeed!" said Nicholas abstractedly.

"As you're perfect in that," resumed Squeers, turning to the boy, "go and look after *my* horse, and rub him down well, or I'll rub you down. The rest of the class go and draw water up, till somebody tells you to leave off, for it's washing-day tomorrow, and they want the coppers filled."

So saying, he dismissed the first class to their experiments in practical philosophy, and eyed Nicholas with a look, half cunning and half doubtful, as if he were not altogether certain what he might think of him by this time.

"That's the way we do it, Nickleby," he said, after a pause.

Nicholas shrugged his shoulders in a manner that was scarcely perceptible, and said he saw it was.

"And a very good way it is, too," said Squeers. "Now, just take them fourteen little boys and hear them some reading, because, you know, you must begin to be useful. Idling about here, won't do."

1 **parlour:** official room where visitors are received 3 **rejoin:** answer, reply 5 **scour:** make a dirty surface clean and bright · **winder:** incorrect spelling of "window" 8 **weed sth.:** Unkraut in etw. jäten 9 **disconcerted:** upset 10 **bottinney:** incorrect spelling of "botany" 20 **quadruped** ['kwɒdrʊped]: four-footed animal 27 **copper:** large pot made of metal, in which one used to boil clothes 29 **cunning:** clever at deceiving or misleading sb.